After the Tax Revolt

After the Tax Revolt:
California's Proposition 13 Turns 30

Jack Citrin and Isaac William Martin, editors

2009
Berkeley Public Policy Press
Institute of Governmental Studies
University of California, Berkeley

Library of Congress Cataloging-in Publication Data

After the tax revolt : California's proposition 13 turns 30 / Jack Citrin, Isaac Martin, editors.
    p. cm.
  ISBN 978-0-87772-430-8
    1. Real property tax—California. 2. Tax and expenditure limitations—California. I. Citrin, Jack. II. Martin, Isaac.

  HJ4191.A68 2009
  336.2209794—dc22

                                  2008054519

Contents

Preface

Isaac William Martin

On June 6, 1978, California voters approved Proposition 13, an initiative amendment to their state constitution that capped local property tax rates, limited the annual increase of local property assessments, converted the local property tax base from market value to acquisition value, required a two-thirds majority of the legislature to enact any state tax increase, and mandated a vote of the people to approve any increase in certain local taxes.

It was a political earthquake. No state had ever approved such a far-reaching constitutional limitation of the power to tax. And Californians did not just approve it; they embraced it, rejecting dire warnings of doomsday from the state's political, business, and academic leaders. Voter turnout was the highest recorded for any off-year election in the history of California and the tax cut won in a landslide, with 65% of the vote. Overnight "Proposition 13" became a buzzword in Washington, D.C., and its anti-tax message the leading mantra in conservative politics. Closer to home, Proposition 13 inaugurated a new era in the governance of California.

Thirty years after its passage, Proposition 13 remains firmly entrenched in California's constitution. It has withstood repeated legal and electoral challenges, including a Supreme Court review. And while its meaning has evolved as it has been further amended by the voters and interpreted by statutes and the courts, its original provisions remain the untouchable third rail of California politics.

Despite or perhaps because of this immutability, Proposition 13 also has become a deeply polarizing symbol. Detractors have at one time or another blamed this constitutional amendment for virtually all of California's ills, from excessive suburban sprawl to earthquake damage to poor performance on standardized tests to child murders. Defenders, for their part, have sometimes credited Proposition 13 with miraculous powers—claiming, for example, that it single-handedly caused all of the economic growth in the Golden State after 1978. Claims like these are a clue that this is a high-stakes policy: people make such assertions about Proposition 13 because they feel passionately about it, and they feel passionately about it because it really does have substantial costs and benefits. But claims like these do not really tell us what the true costs and benefits are.

On June 6, 2008, we assembled the contributors to this volume to take a sober look at the legacy of Proposition 13 on its thirtieth anniversary. Our purpose was neither to praise Proposition 13 nor to bury it. Instead, we sought to summarize the state of our knowledge about the consequences of this critical event in the history of California and the United States. Our contributors included experts from government, the private sector, and the academy. They included economists, sociologists, and political scientists, alongside lawyers, journalists, and policy experts. Their mandate was a simple one: assess what we have learned about the political, economic, and fiscal consequences of Proposition 13 over the last 30 years.

The result is the book that you hold in your hands. This collection of chapters collectively constitutes a cutting-edge and timely review of one of the most important reforms in California history. We think that it will be useful to everyone who cares about California politics—from long-time practitioners to first-time students.

The Benefit of Hindsight

Thirty years bring the benefit of hindsight. The first generation of scholarship to follow Proposition 13 suggested that it did not have much effect beyond cutting property taxes. Commentators drew this conclusion because the short-term trends—in tax revenues, public services, and economic performance—fell short of the catastrophe predicted by some of the initiative's opponents. But time has provided more data and better methods. The best scholarship today does not evaluate the effect of Proposition 13 by comparing it to campaign rhetoric; instead, it uses comparative and statistical methods to test whether the economy and the public budget of California are different than they would have been in the absence of Proposition 13. Scholars who take this approach generally conclude that this constitutional amendment did indeed have a substantial effect on California's economy and public finances.

The three decades since 1978 have been a period of ferment in California's fiscal constitution. Indeed, since Proposition 13 passed, California voters have amended their constitution on average almost once a year, and many of these constitutional changes concern the process of public budgeting. Yet even in moments of severe fiscal crisis, no one has suggested a full-scale effort to repeal Proposition 13.

The primary reason that Proposition 13 persists unchanged is that it remains very popular. Indeed, new public opinion data described by Mark DiCamillo in Chapter One show that it was almost as popular in June 2008 as it was in June 1978. The people who support it the most strongly are, unsurprisingly, long-term homeowners—in other words, those who benefit the most from acquisition-value assessment. But most other people support it too. Indeed, by some measures, Proposition 13 enjoys greater support than ever: although fewer people know of the policy or have an opinion about it today, among those who *do* have an opinion, the margin of those who say they would vote for Proposition 13 over those who say they would vote against it is greater today than the actual margin of victory in 1978.

To understand why this constitutional amendment remains so popular, it may help to understand why voters approved it in the first place. Scholars have completed probably dozens of studies of this question—using aggregate voting data, public opinion surveys, in-depth interviews, and detailed analyses of the documentary record. We have learned a great deal about the political movement that led to this tax limitation. The most important debate today is between those who argue that Proposition 13 was a reaction to rising property assessments, and those who see it instead as a reaction to court-ordered school finance equalization.

Many scholars now argue that Proposition 13 was a response to rising property taxes. Jack Citrin summarizes the argument in the Introduction. According to this view, the legislature undermined support for the property tax by passing a 1967 law called A.B. 80. The new law curbed corruption by requiring local officials to assess homes at a uniform fraction of their current market value. The result was that homeowners saw their property taxes increase whenever home prices increased—and they supported Proposition 13 because it broke the link between rising prices and rising taxes. If this view is correct, then one reason that Proposition 13 remains popular may be that it provides homeowners with stable protection against inflation in real estate values: whatever happens in the housing market property taxes can only increase by 2% a year and most other taxes are subject to supermajority voting.

Other scholars believe that Proposition 13 was a response to the equalization of school finances. This view is represented in Chapter Six by William Fischel, who pioneered this argument in 1989, and developed the underlying theory in a series of subsequent publications. According to this view, it was the decision of the California Supreme Court in *Serrano v. Priest* to redistribute property taxes among school districts that undermined support for the property tax. Homeowners supported property taxes as long as those taxes paid for *local* schools, because well-financed local schools were good for their property values. But once property taxes were to be redistributed away from local schools to *other* districts, many voters who had previously opposed property-tax limitation swung in favor of Proposition 13. Fischel's contribution to this volume restates his thesis, and provides an up-to-date summary of the evidence for it. As Fischel points out, if his view is correct, then the continued popularity of Proposition 13 may rest on the system of statewide equalization funding for school districts—and reforming California school finance to permit greater inequality among districts may be a necessary first step to any reform of Proposition 13.

These perspectives have different implications for what keeps Proposition 13 in place. We can also learn more about this question by attending to the consequences of this initiative—for local governments, state government, businesses, and California homeowners.

The Consequences of Proposition 13

Who were the winners and losers? Howard Jarvis, one of the authors of the amendment, presented it as a victory of "taxpayers" over "government." But this turns out to be a poor description of who won and who lost. As the contributors to this volume illustrate, there is no hard and fast line dividing the taxpayers from beneficiaries of government largesse: all of us pay at least some taxes, and all of us receive at least some benefit from state and local government. The question is how Proposition 13 has changed the distribution of these costs and benefits.

Our contributors offer some surprising answers. David Doerr, in Chapter Five, argues that the costs to some groups are less than you might think. Most local governments lost property tax revenue—but a few cities actually get *more* property tax revenue as a consequence of Proposition 13's requirement that the property tax be "apportioned according to law." Many people believe that Proposition 13 shifted the property tax burden from commercial and industrial property onto owner-occupied homes—but Doerr argues that without the acquisition value provision of Proposition 13, this tax shift would have been even greater. Everyone knows that Proposition 13 reduced reliance on property tax revenues—but Doerr argues that it also made the property tax a *more reliable* revenue source for local government, by stabilizing tax revenues during downturns in the real estate market. Business bears a greater share of a lesser burden.

Some of us may also bear the costs in the form of reduced public services. Jean Ross, in Chapter Nine, focuses on a different provision of Proposition 13— the clause requiring a two-thirds legislative supermajority to increase state taxes. She argues that the costs of this provision are borne by new Californians, who do not have the same opportunities as the generation that voted for Proposition 13. She argues that changes in the economy since Proposition 13 require greater investment in education and infrastructure so that a younger, ethnically diverse generation of Californians can compete effectively. These investments, she argues, are not possible without tax increases that are blocked by Proposition 13.

Who benefits? Terri Sexton, in Chapter Seven, and Steven Sheffrin, in Chapter Eight, summarize and update their authoritative study of this question. Sheffrin argues that the acquisition value provisions of Proposition 13 provide a substantial subsidy to people whose homes would be assessed at a higher value under a market value system. He shows that the amount of this subsidy is variable—it is worth more during housing booms than during recessions, and it is worth more the less frequently you move. On average, it is most valuable for low-income and elderly homeowners, because they move less often than other homeowners. But not all low-income and elderly people benefit, and many people who are not in these groups find Proposition 13 quite valuable indeed.

Sexton asks whether the benefits of acquisition value taxation discourage people from moving. She summarizes a substantial body of research that suggests the answer is yes, although the magnitude of the effect is hard to quantify. Reduced mobility may have positive externalities—for example, it may help to create a sense of community when residents stay put. But Sexton points out that we should also be concerned about negative externalities, which could include increasing commute times, unresponsive local governments, and an overall reduction in the efficiency of the housing market. The distributional consequences of all of these externalities are unknown and probably complex.

The picture is more complicated still when we turn our attention to the spillover effects of Proposition 13 on other public policies. Isaac Martin argues in Chapter Three that most studies underestimate the impact of Proposition 13 because they ignore how it inspired similar policies in other jurisdictions. Other contributors argue that Proposition 13 had spillover effects on other policies even within California. For example, the limitation on property tax revenues caused state and local governments to turn to other revenue sources, including income taxes, sales taxes, and the state lottery. These policies, in turn, may have indirect consequences. Kirk Stark points out in Chapter Ten that the reliance on a retail sales tax to pay for local government leads California's cities and counties to engage in fierce competition to attract retail businesses. David Gamage points out in Chapter Four that the shift toward income tax has made the state budget more volatile with respect to the business cycle. Public revenues expand automatically when our economy is booming and shrink automatically when it is in recession. The result, Gamage argues, is that we tend to schedule our toughest budget debates for those times of economic crisis when they will be hardest to resolve—and the ensuing conflicts prolong the budget process, hurt our state's credit rating, and thereby impose unnecessary costs on everyone who pays taxes in California.

The overall picture, then, is a public policy regime of almost Rube-Goldberg-like complexity. Opponents of Proposition 13 might find something here to like; but even partisans of Proposition 13 will agree that our current fiscal constitution is not working smoothly. Almost every Californian can find something in our post–Proposition-13 fiscal constitution that they might like to reform.

The Future of Proposition 13

For better or for worse, the evidence of this volume suggests that reform will be hard. Some of our contributors argue for selective amendments to Proposition 13. Ross singles out the supermajority clause, and suggests that it might be necessary to repeal this provision to overcome the perennial political gridlock over the state budget. However, Mark Dicamillo's poll, conducted at the height of a fiscal crisis and budgetary stalemate, found that a solid majority of Californians favor retaining the two-thirds requirement for passing the state budget. Sheffrin suggests that the idea of a classified property tax (or the "split roll") might be a politically feasible way to retain the benefits of Proposition 13 while permitting increased property tax revenues. This reform would retain Proposition 13 for homes, but would permit state and local government to raise property taxes on commercial and industrial property and might have negative effects on the willingness of businesses to locate in the state.

Other contributors propose policy changes that would leave Proposition 13 intact. Joel Fox, in the Conclusion, suggests that the solution to California's budget deficit is to rein in spending rather than increasing taxes. John Fund, in Chapter Two, proposes a restoration of the so-called Gann limit, which would restrict the rate of increase in state spending. In a very different vein, Kirk Stark proposes a local income tax as a way to restore a measure of local control. He points out that this reform is possible without further amending the state constitution. By contrast, David Gamage, in Chapter Four, proposes additional constitutional amendments—but amendments that would leave Proposition 13 intact, while avoiding the worst consequences of budget gridlock in Sacramento. He suggests that we might require ballot initiatives to be revenue neutral, so that California voters cannot simply go on increasing the deficit by raising spending and cutting taxes. He also proposes a new system of "budgetary auto-adjusters"—in effect, a default budget that would go into effect in the event of impasse.

As this book goes to press, California faces a grim fiscal prospect. We may be on the verge of a state and local fiscal crisis of a magnitude that has not been seen since the Great Depression. The collapse of housing prices and the wave of foreclosures mean that for the first time since the passage of Proposition 13 property tax revenues are shrinking along with the state's tax from income and sales taxes. There is no question that bold action will be necessary. Whatever direction California's leaders can agree on, they will have to reckon with the legacy of Proposition 13.

Proposition 13 and the Transformation of California Government

Jack Citrin[1]

They say that nothing is forever. Except, perhaps, Proposition 13. Thirty years after voters ushered in the tax revolt by passing this initiative, the fiscal noose it placed around the neck of California government is not much looser. Proposition 13 is indeed the third rail of California government. In the throes of the budget crisis of 2008 and increasing fiscal disarray, there was no serious talk of reforming the property tax system. Proposition 13 was opposed by the elite, supported by the masses. And as Mark DiCamillo reports elsewhere in this book, popular attitudes have hardly changed in 30 years, despite substantial change in the composition of the electorate and years of handwringing about the effects of the measure on public education and other government services. This book's review of the effects of Proposition 13 on California suggests that what fairly can be labeled a revolutionary event neither ushered in the millennium promised by its promoters nor brought on the apocalypse prophesied by its detractors. What did change was the way of doing political business in California. Power shifted from local governments to the state, from the legislature to the governor, and from representative democracy to plebiscitary government.

---

[1] Jack Citrin is Heller Professor of Political Science at the University of California, Berkeley, and director of UC Berkeley's Institute of Governmental Studies.

Genesis

The seed for Proposition 13 was planted in 1965 when it was revealed that elected tax assessors were receiving "campaign contributions" from interested parties as they "reviewed and adjusted" assessments on business properties. Spurred by the outcry over this scandal, the legislature passed A.B. 80 in 1967. This law required communities to reassess all property at 25% within three years and then to conduct subsequent reassessments often enough to keep the ratio intact. No good deed goes unpunished. The unintended consequence of this reform was to increase the assessment for homeowners. Previously, commercial properties as a whole had been assessed at a higher ratio of market value than single-family housing. The application of the uniform rate meant that homeowners had to assume a greater share of the burden if the overall level of property tax revenues was to be maintained. And because residential property tended to turn over more quickly and assessors employed sales prices to establish the market value of similar properties, as long as real estate prices moved upward, shortening the reassessment cycle also added to the relative burden of homeowners.

In the 1970s, reform in the name of good government forbade the use of political discretion as a buffer between homeowners and inflation. For the tax collector, the ideal tax is neither seen nor felt, just collected. The property tax was the opposite: collected twice a year in large and increasing chunks. In the aftermath of A.B. 80 and rising property taxes, the Los Angeles County Tax Assessor sponsored initiatives in 1968 and 1972 to cut property taxes, to assign responsibility of all nonproperty-related services such as health, education, and welfare to the state government and, in the case of the second initiative, to increases sales and sin taxes. The state's political and business leaders, including then-Governor Reagan, opposed Philip Watson's initiatives and both were defeated, but not before the passage of legislation provided for homeowner exemptions and some limits on tax rates. Still, despite evidence of popular discontent neither Watson nor Paul Gann could collect enough signatures to put a new tax limitation measure on the ballot. So Proposition 13 must be viewed as a dramatic swing in the fortunes of the anti-tax movement.

Macroeconomic Change

Inflation was the carrier of the anti-tax spirit through the body politic. With the new assessment procedures in place, the boom in California real estate beginning in 1974 meant that rising values quickly were registered in higher tax bills. By 1977–78, property taxes in California were about 52% above the national norm. And inflation also contributed to the rise in the amount of sales and income taxes paid. While inflation and nominal incomes were increasing, a stagnant national economy stalled corresponding growth in real incomes. The result was bracket creep. People paid more in federal and state taxes, and elected politicians failed to compensate by lowering tax rates. Between 1975 and 1978, while personal income grew by 23%, total state taxes rose by 40%, with the largest increase (48%) in personal income taxes.

So there is no great mystery about a primary cause of the tax revolt. It was higher taxes. People singled out the property tax as particularly onerous; in 1978, a poll found that 60 percent of homeowners said the amount they were paying was unfair. But Proposition 13 also appealed to those who did not pay property taxes directly by requiring a two-thirds majority for the imposition of any new taxes.

Political Disenchantment

As taxes were increasing, so were government spending and the size of public bureaucracies. Big government is a familiar demon in American political culture, and Howard Jarvis made government waste and inefficiency a theme in the campaign for Proposition 13. His sallies echoed during a period when public faith in the integrity and competence of all national institutions was declining. All national and state surveys showed a steady rise in political cynicism in the mid-1970s. More and more people said they only rarely trusted the government to do what is right and agreed that government was run on behalf of a few big interests rather than the people as a whole. President Carter used these data to speak about a national malaise. In California, popular disillusionment was accentuated by the failure of state government to deal with the obvious problem of escalating property taxes. In fact, Jarvis and Gann began circulating petitions for 13 only after the legislature's efforts to pass a tax relief measure in the 1977 session collapsed. Democrats and Republicans squabbled over how much tax relief to provide and the extent to which it should be targeted to low- and moderate-income families. With an election approaching, how to apportion political credit for a tax cut became an issue. Republicans suspected Governor Brown of allowing a surplus to accumulate in order to time a rebate to coincide with a reelection and the governor's own aloofness from the legislature made it hard for him to forge a consensual solution.

Only with the campaign for Proposition 13 underway did the legislature act, producing a proposal for a split roll and a tax cut about half of that proposed by Jarvis-Gann. This proposal appeared on the ballot as Proposition 8 and was denounced by Howard Jarvis as a cruel and cynical hoax the politicians were foisting on voters. One could vote for both measures, assuring oneself half a loaf. But in the end Prop. 13 passed by a 65 to 35 margin, while Prop. 8 was rejected by a margin of 53 to 37.

The Campaign

Proposition 13 had a natural base of support among disgruntled homeowners, but its organizational resources were slight compared to the opposition's. The United Organization of Taxpayers, led by Jarvis, grafted their campaign onto local taxpayer and homeowners associations, mainly in southern California, and ultimately obtained financial support from some large developers and businesses. Nevertheless, arrayed against them were the governor, Speaker of the Assembly, state superintendent of schools, every local school official, prominent Republicans like Pete Wilson and George Deukmejian, large corporations like the Bank of America, Standard Oil, and Southern California Gas and Electric, the AFL-CIO, and the California State Employees Association.

The opposition campaign centered on the "devastating" consequences of the massive tax relief Proposition 13 would provide. Local services, especially public education, would be emasculated. There would be about 250,000 public sector jobs lost statewide and a resultant economic slowdown. The state surplus, whose size was downplayed, was not large enough to compensate for lost revenues, so other taxes would have to be raised. The prudent thing to do was to pass Proposition 8, which provided homeowners with relief and did not lock the state into a situation where needed future adjustments in tax rates would be impossible.

Jarvis's response was pungent. Lower taxes would stimulate rather than retard growth. Eliminating waste and the state surplus could compensate for lost revenue and assure that "needed services" would remain available. "And if a library here and there has to close Wednesday mornings between 9 and 11, life will go on. Who the hell goes to the library in the morning, anyway?" What mattered was to cut taxes and teach government a lesson.

The Field Poll showed that from February to May, about half the public said they favored Prop. 13, about one-third said they opposed it, and the rest were undecided. When respondents were read the standard arguments both for and against the measure, approval tended to decline by about 10%. In other words, some positive opinions were soft. And an April Field Poll showed Proposition 8 running slightly ahead of 13.

What changed the dynamic of the campaign and assured victory for Prop. 13 were the following climactic events. On May 16, "city officials" in Los Angeles announced that the new assessments would show that the total assessed valued of the property in the city had increased by 17.5% in just one year. Since only one-third of all property was reassessed each year, this meant that the average increase per reassessment would be far higher and many people faced the prospect of a tax bill double the previous year. The same day, Alexander Pope, the L.A. country tax assessor announced that voters could find out immediately how their property had been assessed rather than waiting until after the election in July. The next day the county board of supervisors ordered him to mail the official reassessment notices before the election.

A firestorm of protest ensued as the media graphically depicted the fear and anger of people anticipating tax bills they could not pay. Within a week, the board of supervisors endorsed a rollback of all assessments to the previous year's levels. This mobilized people who had been reassessed in the previous two years and now felt they were being treated unfairly. On May 26, Governor Brown, sensitive as ever to the tide of public opinion, proposed a statewide freeze on reassessments, but was forced to abandon the idea five days later. In the meantime, the polls recorded a spectacular increased in support for Proposition 13. The furor in Los Angeles was a godsend for the pro-13 campaign. It concentrated public attention on the reality of rising taxes and drowned out warnings of lost services. The confused and contradictory responses of politicians seemed to validate the charge that they were unable or unwilling to provide tax relief. In the words of Yogi Berra, one week before the election itself it was over. The fat lady had sung.

Deconstructing the Vote

Tax Revolt, a book I co-authored with David Sears, is subtitled "Something for Nothing in California." By this we were referring to an entrenched pattern of opinion. People want to pay less in taxes; a majority also says it prefers a smaller government, even if this means fewer services. But when asked whether government should spend more or less on a particular category of service, an overwhelming majority consistently says more for everything except welfare and "administration." Indeed, the most popular services, fire, police, and education, are the most labor intensive, have highly paid unionized employees, and thus are very expensive.

Tax relief was the main motivation of support for Prop. 13. In 1978 as now, owners were more supportive than renters, and the level of voting for Proposition 13 rose in tandem with the amount of anticipated tax savings. Public sector employees were more opposed than private sector employees. The elderly also were stronger supporters of Proposition 13 than the relatively young. And whites were more likely to vote for the initiative than blacks.

There also were predictable political underpinnings of the vote: Republicans were more supportive than Democrats; conservatives more pro-13 than self-described liberals or moderates, and people who said they preferred a smaller government were more in favor of the property tax reform than those who wanted the government to provide more services even if it meant higher taxes. Political cynicism, as indexed by expressions of mistrust in government and the belief that waste was rampant, also boosted support for Proposition 13.

The Aftermath

Soon after the passage of Proposition 13, the state legislature, burdened with an embarrassingly large surplus of $11 billion, cut state taxes by more than $1 billion by providing a one-time income tax credit, increasing tax relief for renters, reducing some business taxes, and partially indexing state income taxes. These reductions were partially designed to head off what became labeled as Jarvis II, a proposal on the June 1980 ballot to cut state personal income taxes by limiting rates to 50% of those in effect in 1978. In part because of the reduction in taxes, and in part because of the fear that this time such a large cut in taxes would lead to devastating cuts in services and public sector jobs, this draconian measure was defeated by a large margin, 61% to 39%.

Two years later, however, tax cutting resumed with the passage of initiatives fully indexing the state income tax, overriding a veto of similar legislation, and fully repealing the state's inheritance tax. In these heady days, voters rejected proposals for a special tax on the state's oil companies and a "tax-simplicity" initiative that would have shifted taxes from individuals to businesses. Proposition 13 and these successor measures thus protected Californian taxpayers from most of the tax consequences of inflation.

Proposition 13 had national repercussions as other states responded to the evidence of public discontent with high taxes in the context of slow economic growth. In most cases, legislatures acted. Isaac Martin provides a detailed account of the spread of the tax revolt. But in the first five years following the passage of Proposition 13, between 1978 and 1982, 43 states acted to cut taxes and limit the growth of expenditures. Clearly, Prop. 13 reinvigorated the initiative process nationwide, and it took on a more professionalized form and spread to other domains of policy, such as welfare reform, school vouchers, auto insurance, gun control, nuclear policy, and environmental protection.

Governing California after Prop. 13

Proposition 13 initiated a new era in California government and public policy. Liberal critics like Peter Schrag are unrelenting in their criticism, pointing mainly to cuts in spending on public schools, health services, and transportation and the concomitant boom in prison construction (Schrag 2004).[2] The proper balance between public and private spending is a value judgment, of course, but some facts are clear. In the past 30 years, California once a high tax and high services state in the rankings of American states moved down both ladders and now is in the middle of both tax and overall spending rankings.

Thanks to Proposition 13, the composition of California's revenue stream has changed. Property taxes are a much smaller share on the total pie, and the

---

[2] Peter Schrag, *Paradise Lost: California's Experience, America's Future.* (Berkeley: Univeristy of California Press, 2004).

state relies heavily on the highly volatile income and sales taxes. As a result, the coffers bulge quickly during booms and empty rapidly during economic downturns. Since the public continues to demand more services and spending formulas, labor contracts, and inflation drive spending upward, California, encumbered by rules that require two-third votes to increase general taxes and pass the state budget, has confronted episodic fiscal crises. Proposition 13 may have slowed the dreadnought of increased government spending but certainly has not reduced the overall size of government.

State and local governments have employed a range of tactics to replace the money seized by the tax revolutionaries: these include the passage of special taxes, especially, parcel taxes, fees and charges for a wide range of services, leasebacks, and bond financing. Taken together, these measures have filled much of the revenue gap engendered by lost property tax revenues; a long-time resident inspecting her annual property tax bill, in Berkeley at least, now sees a long list of charges for special taxes and bonds that together approximate the levy for the traditional property tax. At the same time, these special taxes and charges have an uncertain future; they depend on voter approval and typically are subject to renewal after a specified period.

After Proposition 13, California moved from representative to plebiscitary government. California adopted direct democracy in 1912. Between 1940 and 1970, there were 42 initiatives on the state ballot. From 1971 to 2005, there were 157 such measures, and the bulk came after the passage of Proposition 13. Moreover, these figures do not count the myriad of local and county ballot measures. As a result of Proposition 13, all major policy decisions in California have been settled by a popular vote or a threat of such a vote. Initiatives are used by segments of the public sector to guarantee their share of the budget. They are the weapon of policy entrepreneurs, such as the actor Rob Reiner and the present governor, Arnold Schwarzenegger, to promote pet projects. They are used by consumer activists to impose rules on business and by business to ward off such efforts. Gubernatorial candidates seek to ride on the coattails of popular initiatives. And of course antipolitical movements, sometimes funded outside the state, have used the initiative to limit the power of elected representatives.

An incomplete list of major post-13 initiatives include reform of inheritance taxes, guaranteeing the public schools a share of the state budget, taxes on tobacco to assure spending for health programs, auto insurance reform, abolishing affirmative action, passing a state lottery, term limits, an income tax surcharge on millionaires, the "three strikes" for convicted felons, and reform of bilingual education. Most of these measures were aimed at the status quo. A number of far-reaching initiatives have failed, of course. Redistricting reform is a good example. In that case, the majority Democrats in the legislature were able to retain control of the process after expensive campaigns in which Hollywood actors played a prominent role.

At the same time, politicians and powerful interest groups have learned to use direct democracy to market policies that could not pass the legislature. Infrastructure bonds are a good example. These are carefully crafted to give a piece of the pie to developers and environmentalists, unions, and the education and medical lobbies. The result is an expensive, complex, and comprehensive proposal that buys off the potential opposition but also raises the cost of doing business. In a sense, the bargaining and coalition-building that used to be a feature of the legislative process now has moved into the arena of direct democracy, stage managed by lobbyists and campaign consultants.

Incredibly complex policy matters are being decided by voters with limited knowledge and it is easy to point to unintended consequences that pose serious adjustment problems. And while the academic and political establishments rail against the excesses of the initiative process, no serous reform seems likely. The mistrust of elected officials that helped fuel Proposition 13 remains intact. Polls continue to show that a large majority of the public wants to retain the voice the initiative provides them and believes that policy made at the ballot box is superior to what would emerge from Sacramento.

Conclusion

Proposition 13 took dead aim at high taxes, fired, and scored a direct hit. Property and other taxes are lower than they would have been had the initiative failed. Prop. 13 essentially provided voters with an inflation security system in an era of escalating home values. It is this reliability, I think, that sustains popular support for the measure. People know what they will pay and even if neighbors who bought at different times have widely divergent tax burdens, this doesn't seem to be too bothersome. I bought later than you, but someone else will buy later than me.

Despite its success in cutting taxes, Proposition 13 had other consequences that even its promoters probably regret. It shifted power from local governments, arguably closer to the people, to the states. It slowed spending but did not halt its growth. And the fiscal constraints on the legislature unleashed a mad scramble for money that has produced an incoherent, dysfunctional system of budgeting that makes it harder to react flexibly in times of fiscal stress. Finally, Proposition 13 boosted the role of direct democracy in deciding public policy. But this has not meant the triumph of grassroots democracy. The initiative now is in the hands of all major players and money matters as much as if not more than ever.

The process began because of failures of the governor and legislature and now the chickens are firmly ensconced. Popular mistrust of California government rages on unabated, and thinking people are considering again the need for wholesale institutional reform. The essays in this book provide a wide-ranging look at the impact of Proposition 13, how California adjusted, and how to think about the future.

Section I. Political Repercussions

Chapter 1

Californians' Views of Proposition 13 Thirty Years after its Passage

Mark DiCamillo[1]

On the occasion of Proposition 13's thirtieth anniversary, The Field Poll teamed with the Institute for Governmental Studies (IGS) to re-examine California voter opinions of the landmark property tax reduction initiative and its major provisions. The poll also updated a number of Field Poll measures about voter attitudes toward taxes and the state's current budget deficit.

IGS Director Jack Citrin and I collaborated in the development of the survey questions. Field Research Corporation conducted the survey by telephone among a random sample of 1,052 California registered voters in English and Spanish from May 17–26, 2008. On a number of questions the overall sample was divided into two approximately equal-sized random subsamples to test for variations in question wording and its effect on voter responses. The findings were publicly released on June 6, 2008, the day of the IGS conference, and are described below.

---

[1] Mark DiCamillo is director of The Field Poll.

Familiarity with Proposition 13

Voter familiarity with Proposition 13 divides into three roughly equal-sized camps. About one-third of voters (37%) report being very familiar with it, another third (30%) are somewhat familiar, while the remaining third (33%) are not too or not at all familiar with it.

Familiarity is directly related to whether a voter is a homeowner or renter. Nearly three times as many homeowners (46%) as renters (16%) report being very familiar with Prop. 13. In addition, *when* a homeowner bought their current home is another major correlate. For example, a much larger proportion (75%) of long-time homeowners (i.e., those who bought their home prior to Prop. 13's passage 30 years ago) are very familiar with the initiative compared to homeowners who purchased their homes in the past five years (29%). See Table 1.

How Californians Would Vote on Prop. 13 Today

Even 30 years after its passage, Prop. 13 remains very popular with voters in California. If Prop. 13 were up for a vote again today, the survey finds that more than twice as many voters (57%) would vote in favor as would vote against it (23%). Another 20% have no opinion. The current two and one-half to one margin in favor is proportionately greater than its actual margin of passage in June 1978, when voters endorsed Prop. 13 by slightly less than a two-to-one margin (65% to 35%).

Homeowners were among Prop. 13's biggest supporters and turned out in record numbers to pass the initiative 30 years ago. Today, support for Prop. 13 among homeowners remains strong, with 64% saying they continue to back the initiative, while just 24% are opposed. Yet, even among renters more favor (41%) than oppose (23%) Prop. 13, although many (36%) have no opinion.

Support for Prop. 13 is greatest among long-time homeowners. Nearly eight in 10 homeowners who bought their present homes prior to the passage of Prop. 13 (79%) would support the initiative if it were up for a vote again today. However, even those who bought their homes more recently (i.e., in the past 10 years), and who constitute about half of all homeowners in the poll, support Prop. 13 by nearly two-to-one margins. This is significant, since many observers had expected that support for Prop. 13 might diminish over time, as long-time homeowners who benefited most from its passage became a smaller share of voters. The results of the current survey do not support that view. See Table 2.

Table 1. Voter Familiarity with Proposition 13 Thirty Years after Its Passage

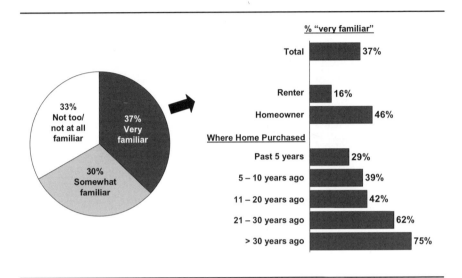

Table 2. Voting Preferences if Proposition 13 Were Up for a Vote Again Today

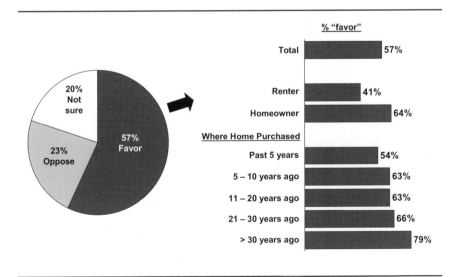

Opinions about Changing Some of Prop. 13's Main Provisions

The poll also asked voters their opinions about a number of proposals that have been made to amend Prop. 13 or change some of its major provisions. Most are rejected by wide margins in the current survey.

For example, a proposal to gradually raise the property taxes of long-time property owners so that the amount they pay is more in line with the amount paid by recent home buyers of similarly valued property is rejected two and one-half to one (66% to 27%). Not only do very large majorities of long-time homeowners oppose this idea, but it is also rejected by a greater than two to one margin (68% to 26%) among those who bought their homes in the past 10 years. See Table 3.

Another of Prop. 13's major provisions was to limit the amount local governments could increase property taxes to no more than 2% each year. When voters are asked whether they approved or disapproved of changing this provision to allow their own local governments to increase property taxes by more than 2% per year, they reject this idea by a greater than four-to-one margin (78% to 17%).

Large majorities of both homeowners and renters disapprove of this proposed change. There is little appetite for changing this provision among registered Republicans, Democrats or nonpartisans. See Table 4.

There is also strong resistance to the idea of changing the Prop. 13 provision that requires a two-thirds vote of the state legislature to increase taxes. This question was posed in two slightly different ways in the current survey. About half of the sample was asked the question after first being reminded that the state was currently facing a large budget deficit ranging between $14 and $20 billion. No mention was made of the state's current budget deficit among the other sample of voters.

The results show that similar large majorities of voters—about seven in ten—disapprove of making this change, regardless of whether the deficit is cited or not. In both cases, opposition includes over six in ten Democrats and nonpartisans and over eight in ten Republicans. See Table 5.

Voters were again divided into two random subsamples and read alternative versions of a question to change Prop. 13 by establishing a split roll method of property taxation, which would tax residential and commercial properties at different rates.

One version asked voters whether they approved or disapproved of changing Prop. 13 "to permit business and commercial property owners to be taxed at a higher rate than owners of residential property," implying a potential tax increase on businesses.

The other version asked voters whether they approved or disapproved of changing Prop. 13 "to permit owners of residential property to be taxed at a lower rate than business and commercial property owners," implying a potential tax reduction for homeowners.

When the issue is posed as a potential tax reduction to homeowners, the idea is endorsed by a greater than two-to-one margin (61% to 28%). However,

Table 3. Change Prop. 13 to Gradually Raise the Property Taxes of Long-Time Property Owners, So the Amount They Pay is More in Line with the Amount Paid by Recent Buyers of Similarly Valued Property

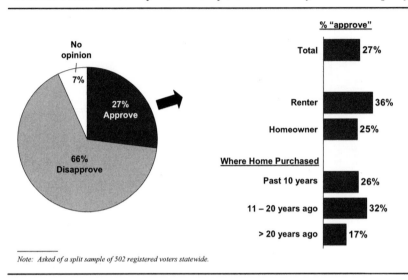

Note: Asked of a split sample of 502 registered voters statewide.

Table 4. Change Prop. 13 to Allow Your Local Government to Increase Property Taxes by More Than 2% Per Year

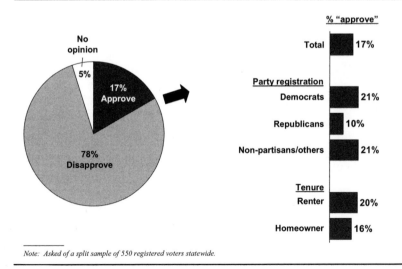

Note: Asked of a split sample of 550 registered voters statewide.

Table 5. Change Prop. 13 to Enable the State Legislature to Increase Taxes by a Simple Majority Vote (with and without mention of the state's current budget situation)

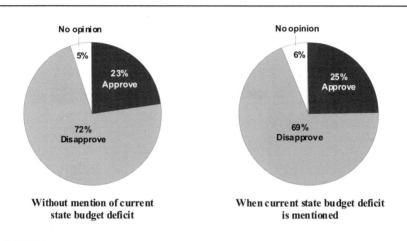

No opinion

5%

23% Approve

72% Disapprove

Without mention of current state budget deficit

No opinion

6%

25% Approve

69% Disapprove

When current state budget deficit is mentioned

Note: Each question asked of a split sample of 502 or 550 registered voters statewide.

when the issue is framed as a potential tax increase on businesses, voters are about evenly divided, with 47% approving and 44% disapproving.

While majorities of Democrats, Republicans, and nonpartisans endorse the idea of enacting a split roll system that results in lower property taxes for homeowners, there are big partisan differences when the issue is framed as a potential property tax increase for businesses. Democrats favor a split roll system that would permit higher property taxes on businesses than residential owners 55% to 34%. However, Republicans are opposed by a nearly equivalent 56% to 36% margin. Nonpartisans are closely divided and mirror the sentiments of the overall voting public, with 46% in favor and 44% opposed. See Table 6.

Trend of Opinion about the Overall Level of State and Local Taxes

The Field Poll has at different intervals over the past 31 years asked cross-sections of Californians their perceptions of the overall level of state and local taxes. This question was posed again in the current survey. The results show that about six in ten voters (61%) now feel that state and local taxes are either much too high or somewhat high, while 37% say they are about right.

Table 6. Change Prop. 13 by Taxing Residential and Commercial Properties at Different Rates (Using Alternative Descriptions of How This Would Be Done)

Tax commercial property at a higher rate than residential property

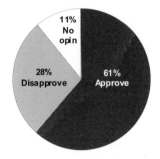

Tax residential property at a lower rate than commercial property

Note: Each question asked of a split sample of either 502 or 550 registered voters statewide.

These findings are close to the poll's 31-year average and are quite similar to those obtained in each Field Poll survey over the past seven years. See Table 7a.

Nearly three in four Republicans (73%) describe the level of state and local taxes as too high, exceeding the proportions of Democrats (55%) and nonpartisans (54%) who say this. In addition, while lower income voters are somewhat more likely than higher income voters to feel taxes are too high, majorities across all income categories feel this way. See Table 7b.

Specific State and Local Taxes Seen as Being Too High

In 1977, prior to Prop. 13's passage, The Field Poll asked Californians to volunteer which specific state or local taxes they felt were too high. At the time, three times as many singled out property taxes (60%) as cited any other single tax.

This measure has been updated intermittently over the past 31 years, with very different outcomes. In 1980, two years after the passage of Prop. 13, the state income tax (42%) was cited by nearly twice as many voters as those mentioning the property tax (23%) in this context. In 1991 more mentioned sales taxes (52%) than any other state and local tax. In 1998 no single tax was singled out more than the others, with about three in ten citing sales taxes (32%), the state income tax (30%) and the state gasoline tax (30%).

Table 7a. Trend of California's Perceptions of the Level of State and Local Taxes (1977–2008)

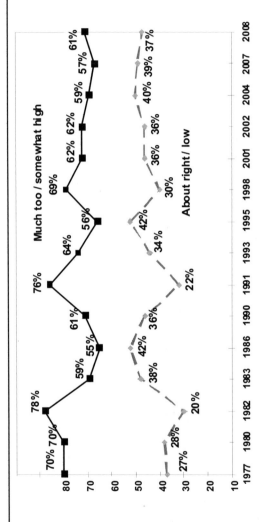

Source: The Field Poll.   *Note:* 1977-1998 measures conducted among all California adults, while 2001-2008 measures conducted among registered voters.

This question was asked using a three-point answer scale (much too high, somewhat high or about right). Most previous measures also used this scale but on occasion a four-point scale (much too high, somewhat high, about right or too low) was employed. When the four-point scale was used, very few respondents chose the "too low" answer alternative. Results from these surveys are included in the trend line because differences in the scale did not materially affect the measures.

Table 7b. Californians' Perception of the Level of State and Local Taxes, 2008 by Subgroup

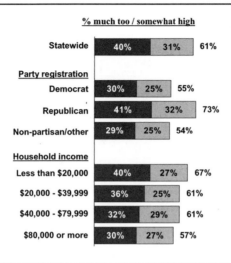

This year, a similar pattern emerges as was observed in 1998. At present, 32% of voters offer the state gasoline tax, 29% cite property taxes, 27% state income taxes, and 22% sales taxes. No other state and local tax is volunteered by more than 9% statewide.

There are some subgroup differences in voter responses to this question, especially regarding those who feel property taxes are too high. Recent homeowners, who on average paid more for their homes and thus are generally paying higher property taxes than their neighbors who bought their homes earlier, are more likely than others to complain that property taxes are too high.

Other subgroup differences include these:
- Southern Californians, especially those living outside of Los Angeles County and Central Valley, are more likely than northern Californians to cite gasoline taxes as being too high.
- High-income earners are more likely than lower income voters to complain about the level of state income taxes.
- Republicans are more likely than Democrats and nonpartisans to play back more than one state and local tax as being too high. See Table 8.

Table 8. Which Specific State or Local Tax is Too High? (volunteered replies) (1977–2008)

	1977	1980	1991	1998	2008
Gasoline tax	10%	26%	12%	30%	32%
Property tax	60	23	22	22	29
State income tax	20	42	26	30	27
Sales tax	17	29	52	32	22
Tobacco tax	1	8	3	11	9
Vehicle registration tax	NC	NC	NC	NC	9
Alcohol tax	10	8	3	9	7
Business/corporation tax	NC	NC	NC	NC	6
Other tax	13	13	15	15	4
None/no answer	11	22	12	26	28

Columns add to more than 100% due to multiple mentions.
NC: Not coded separately with answers included in "other tax" category.

More or Fewer Government Services

Voters were also asked whether state and local governments should provide more or fewer services to the public. A split sample approach was employed on this question. About half of voters were asked about the level of government services with no mention made of their possible impact on taxes. The other half were asked whether they wanted more government services *even if it means raising your taxes and fees* or fewer services *if this means that your taxes and fees will be kept at or below current levels.*

The results show stark differences in voter response between the two alternatives. Twice as many voters prefer government providing more (61%) rather than fewer (30%) services when the question is posed without any reference to taxes. However, when voters are reminded of the potential impact that the level of government services could have on taxes, opinions are about evenly divided with 44% preferring more government services and 40% opting for fewer government services.

Large majorities of Republicans favor government providing fewer rather than more services in both contexts. On the other hand, there is a significant drop-off in the proportion of Democrats and nonpartisans favoring more government services when the issue of taxes is raised. Whereas nearly eight in ten Democrats (79%) and nearly seven in ten nonpartisans (68%) prefer more government services when taxes are not referenced, when they are, support drops to small majorities of 56% and 51%, respectively.

The views of white non-Hispanic voters also differ markedly from those of Latinos and African Americans on this issue. Among white non-Hispanics a slim 51% majority supports more government services when taxes are not referenced, but this declines to 40% when the potential impact of taxes is raised. By contrast, greater than seven in ten African Americans favor more government services in both settings. Latinos also support an expanded government in both settings, but by varying margins. Greater than eight in ten (84%) say this when taxes are not referenced, but this declines to 54% when asked about this in the context of potentially higher taxes. See Table 9.

Dealing with the State's Budget Deficit

Several questions probed voter opinions about the state's current budget deficit. The first asked voters whether they felt the deficit should be closed mostly through spending cuts or mostly through tax increases. By a greater than two to one margin, voters prefer closing the deficit mostly through spending cuts (63%) than mostly through tax increases (26%).

Republicans are more likely than other voters to prefer reducing the deficit mostly through spending cuts, with 80% favoring this approach. Support for closing the deficit mostly through spending cuts drops to 64% among nonpartisans and to just 49% among Democrats. See Table 10.

Underlying voter preferences for spending cuts is the belief that the state can continue to provide roughly the same level of services that it currently does even if its budget had to be cut by $14 to $20 billion. Statewide 66% of voters subscribe to this view, while just 29% disagree. Majorities of Democrats (59%), Republicans (77%) and nonpartisans (63%) agree with this contention. See Table 11.

Notwithstanding this view or the preference that most voters have for closing the deficit mostly through spending cuts, greater than eight in ten voters (81%) expect that in the end the state budget deficit will likely involve some form of tax increase. Just 14% feel otherwise. There is broad consensus about this among Democrats, Republicans and nonpartisans. See Table 12.

Voters were also asked about their preferences for cutting specific program areas. Five areas of state spending were posed to voters in this context in random order. The areas cited were the public schools, higher education, health care programs, prisons and corrections, and public assistance programs. The overall sample was divided into two random subsamples on this issue. About half of the voters were asked which category they would be most willing to cut to avoid a tax increase, while the other half were asked which spending category they would not want cut even if it resulted in a tax increase.

The results show prisons and corrections to be the program area that the largest proportion of voters (47%) favors cutting to avoid a tax increase. Next most

Table 9. Should state and local government provide more or fewer services to the public (with and without mention of its impact on taxes)

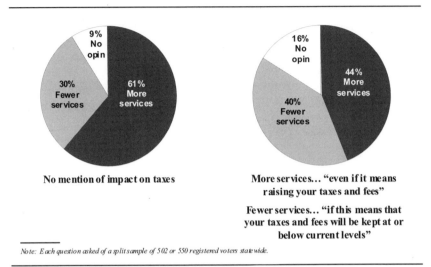

No mention of impact on taxes

More services... "even if it means raising your taxes and fees"

Fewer services... "if this means that your taxes and fees will be kept at or below current levels"

Note: Each question asked of a split sample of 502 or 550 registered voters statewide.

Table 10. Should the State's Current Budget Deficit Be Dealt with Mostly through Spending Cuts or Mostly through Tax Increases?

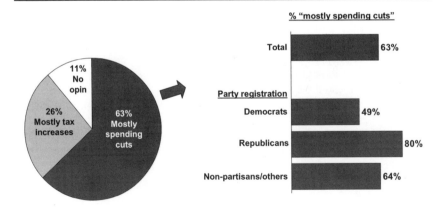

Note: Asked of a split sample of 502 registered voters statewide.

Table 11. Agree/Disagree: ". . . the State Can Provide Roughly the Same Level of Services That It Currently Does, Even if Its Budget Has to Be Cut by $14-20 Billion"

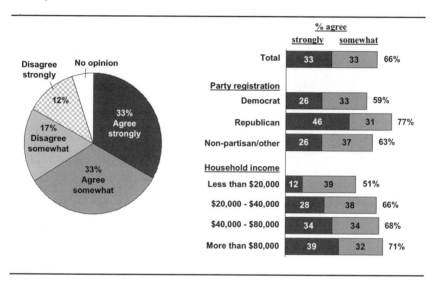

Table 12. In the End, Will the State Resolve Its Current Budget Deficit with or without an Increase in Taxes?

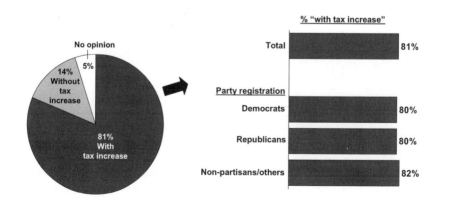

Note: Question asked of a split sample of 502 registered voters statewide.

frequently cited is public assistance programs (23%). None of the three other spending categories receives more than 8% mention in this setting.

By contrast, public schools is the spending category that more voters (37%) feel shouldn't be cut even if it resulted in a tax increase. Next most frequently mentioned is health care programs (25%), followed by higher education at 14%. Few voters cite prisons and corrections or public assistance programs in this context.

There are significant differences in the preferences of Democrats and Republicans regarding which of the five spending categories they would most prefer cutting to avoid a tax increase. Democrats and nonpartisans are much more inclined to mention prisons and corrections than any other category, with greater than half choosing this category. By contrast, more Republicans prefer making cuts to public assistance programs (35%) than prisons and corrections (32%). See Table 13.

A final set of questions asked voters their reactions to a set of hypothetical trade-off questions relating to the level of taxes they would be willing to pay and to reductions in services they would be willing to accept in two state program areas, the K-12 schools and the state prisons.

The first question asked voters whether or not they would be willing to accept larger K-12 class sizes if this meant taxes could be kept at about current levels. The results show that by a nearly two-to-one margin (60% to 37%) voters reject this trade-off. While Republicans are about evenly divided on this question, Democrats and nonpartisans oppose this idea by greater than two-to-one margins. In addition, a larger proportion of voters living in households where a family member attends school oppose this idea than voters where no family member attends a school. See Table 14.

Voters were next asked whether they would be willing to pay an additional $100 or $200 per year in taxes if this meant that the average K-12 class size would be reduced. A nearly two-to-one majority would support paying an additional $100 per year in this scenario. Support drops to a narrower five-to-four margin (54% to 42%) when the amount of tax in question is raised to $200 per year. See Table 15.

Two different types of trade-off questions were also asked with regard to the state prisons. The first asked voters their willingness to allow the early release of up to 50,000 nonviolent prisoners from the state prisons if this kept taxes from going up by either $100 or $200 per year. The results show majority support for these proposals. See Table 16.

On the other hand, majorities of voters are opposed to the idea of paying an additional $100 or $200 per year in taxes if this meant not releasing up to 50,000 nonviolent prisoners from state prisons. The idea of paying an additional $100 per year to avoid this is opposed by a 54% to 42% margin. Opposition grows to nearly two to one (63% to 32%) if this meant paying an additional $200 per year in taxes. See Table. 17.

Table 13. Areas of State Spending Voters Are Most Willing to Cut and Most Willing to Protect from Budget Cutbacks

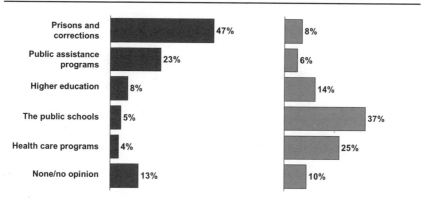

	Cut spending to avoid a tax increase	Don't cut even if it means a tax increase
Prisons and corrections	47%	8%
Public assistance programs	23%	6%
Higher education	8%	14%
The public schools	5%	37%
Health care programs	4%	25%
None/no opinion	13%	10%

Responses to this question were limited only to these five areas of state spending.
Note: Question asked of a split sample of 502 or 550 registered voters statewide.

Table 14. Willingness to Accept Larger K-12 Class Sizes if This Meant Taxes Could be Kept at about Current Levels

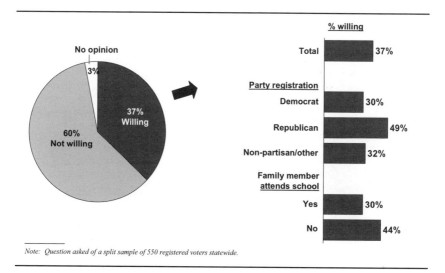

% willing

No opinion	3%
37% Willing	
60% Not willing	

	% willing
Total	37%
Party registration	
Democrat	30%
Republican	49%
Non-partisan/other	32%
Family member attends school	
Yes	30%
No	44%

Note: Question asked of a split sample of 550 registered voters statewide.

Table 15. Willingness to Pay an Additional ($100) ($200) Per Year in Taxes if This Meant Average K-12 School Class Sizes Would Be Reduced

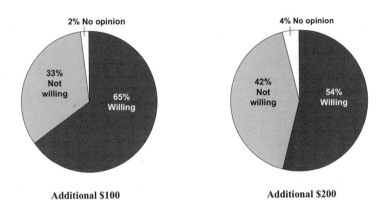

Additional $100   **Additional $200**

Note: Each question asked of a split sample of 502 or 550 registered voters statewide.

Table 16. Willingness to Allow Early Release of up to 50,000 Nonviolent Prisoners from State Prisons If This Kept Your Taxes from Going Up By ($100) ($200) Per Year

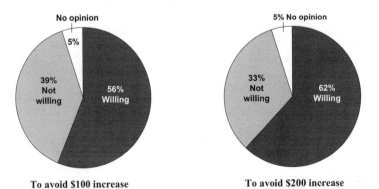

To avoid $100 increase   **To avoid $200 increase**

Note: Each question asked of a split sample of 502 or 550 registered voters statewide.

Table 17. Willingness to Pay an Additional ($100) ($200) Per Year in Taxes if This Meant *Not* Releasing Up to 50,000 Nonviolent Prisoners from State Prisons

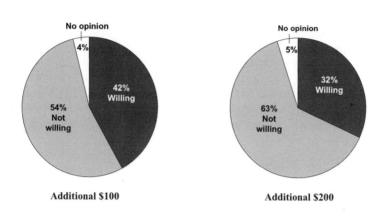

Note: *Each question asked of a split sample of 502 or 550 registered voters statewide.*

Conclusion

Proposition 13 remains very popular with California voters 30 years after its passage. More than twice as many voters (57%) say they would vote in favor of Prop. 13 if it were up for a vote again today, while just 23% are opposed. Homeowners, who were among the initiative's biggest supporters in 1978, remain strongly supportive. Even a two-to-one majority of homebuyers who bought their houses within the past 10 years say they would back Prop.13 if voting on it today.

Voters also oppose altering many of Prop. 13's main provisions. For example, large majorities reject proposals to gradually increase the property taxes of long-time homeowners so they are more in line with the amount paid by more recent homebuyers, to raise the 2% per year limit on how much local governments can increase property taxes, or to change Prop. 13's two-thirds vote requirement in the state legislature to increase taxes.

One Prop. 13 provision that receives the highest level of support for modifying relates to establishing a split roll property tax system, whereby businesses and commercial properties would be taxed at a higher rate than residential property. But, even here, there is no consensus, with 47% supportive and 44% opposed.

The poll identifies a number of factors contributing to Prop. 13's continuing popularity. One relates to the fact that most voters (61%) have not significantly changed their view that state and local taxes in California are much too high or somewhat high. Another is that the property tax is among the most often mentioned tax when asked which state or local taxes are too high. Third, voters are much more supportive of closing the state's current budget deficit "mostly through spending cuts" (63%) rather than "mostly through tax increases" (23%), so there is not a strong appetite for tax increases.

Finally, the survey demonstrates anew voters' long-held, albeit somewhat paradoxical, view that state funding levels can be cut substantially without significantly impacting the level of services government provides. In the current survey 63% believe the state budget can be cut by as much as $14 to $20 billion while still providing roughly the same level of services that it currently does.

Chapter 2

Proposition 13: A Watershed Moment Bridging FDR and Reagan

John Fund[1]

Proposition 13 had a profound impact in my life. It taught me an awful lot about politics and governance in one short summer.

In 1978, I was an intern in the California State Legislature. In late May, Paul Priolo, who was the Assembly Republican leader, told his caucus members he had just come back from a town hall meeting in his Ventura County district. "I've been holding these town hall meetings for years," he told them. "I was there to explain to them that Prop. 13 would be a disaster, reminding them that out of 120 California state legislators, only four endorsed it." But Priolo said his message didn't sell. "I stood up before 800 people, the greatest number that had ever shown up at a town hall meeting, and I said to them if Prop. 13 passed it would decimate local services. It would destroy their schools. It would lead to disaster. I said that if they voted for it it would end local government as they knew it." The reaction he got stunned him. "I got my first standing ovation, ever," he recounted. "I knew something was wrong." He then looked at his fellow Republicans and said, "Guys and gals, we're in trouble. It's time for us to follow, not to lead."

---

[1] John Fund is a columnist for the *Wall Street Journal.*

That event taught me something very valuable in politics. Our political leaders say they're leaders. In reality, they're mostly followers, and that applies to both political parties.

Proposition 13 had a profound impact nationally. Not only did it set off a nationwide tax revolt, but a very careful student of California politics was paying attention. Ronald Reagan may have opposed or stood silent when a series of property tax reform measures were unsuccessfully proposed in the 1970s. But after Prop. 13's landslide win, he decided to make tax reduction the centerpiece of his presidential campaign in 1980. He embraced Kemp-Roth, a dramatic cutting of marginal income tax rates. He won; he implemented Kemp-Roth and changed much of America's fiscal history.

The political success of Prop. 13 has made it difficult for people to view it objectively. One of the hardest things in politics is trying to understand voting trends you profoundly disagree with. That goes for both sides of the political spectrum.

In 1929, we had a crisis of capitalism, the Great Depression. We could argue about its sources and its causes and how much the New Deal helped recovery. But regardless of that debate, it is clear Franklin Delano Roosevelt was elected to do something about people's suffering.

People were very insecure in their lives, especially senior citizens. Seniors are very concerned about security, and they vote in much higher numbers than the general population. Roosevelt tapped into that. A cornerstone of the New Deal was the 1935 Social Security program, a social safety net for those people in their retirement years. The average age of death at that time was 65, so Roosevelt was very cleverly proposing a program that most people wouldn't benefit from. He didn't foresee the great life expectancy increases we enjoy today. But it nonetheless proved to be an extremely popular program.

Conservative Republicans hated this program. Business hated it because rather than have the taxpayer pay all of the cost, half of it was disguised as an employer tax, even though ultimately it was going to be passed on in the form of lower wages to employees.

For 40 or 50 years after its passage, an unstated—and sometimes stated—goal of many conservatives was to undermine and ultimately roll back Social Security. The Republican Party kept running up against the rocks and being destroyed because of this goal. It became the third rail of American politics. What people did not understand, if they were conservative critics of the program, was that Social Security had become a basic tenet of our social safety net, and it was not going to be touched. It could be supplemented. You could certainly have 401(k) plans and IRAs, but Social Security was inviolate.

If anyone was in any doubt about that, they were disabused in 2005 when President George W. Bush broached the idea of allowing workers to invest part of their payroll tax payments in mutual funds and relatively safe investments in the stock market to get a higher return. That went nowhere so fast; it never even got a vote in a House or Senate committee. It went much less further than even Hillary Clinton's healthcare reform plan of 1994.

Now it's true that 25 nations have adopted private pension programs, but all of them are parliamentary democracies, a far different mechanism by which to effect social change than we have. I think there is a future in expanded private pensions, but the basic Social Security system is inviolate.

I submit that Proposition 13 has taken on many of the same characteristics and political bulletproofing as Social Security. In the 1970s, we didn't have a crisis of capitalism as we did in the Great Depression. We had a crisis of government. After Vietnam, after Watergate, after the Great Society programs were seen as failures or not fulfilling their promise, there was a crisis of confidence in government. As a result, when property taxes went sky-high in the 1970s, people reacted against that, especially senior citizens seeking security, especially people who were fearful that they would be forced out of their homes by rising property taxes. They sought security. Prop. 13, in its own way, was a search for security, just as much as the search for Social Security was a desire for security for people in their old age. People say their home is their castle. One of the biggest things that matter to people in their golden years is the safety of their home.

So I think opponents of Prop. 13 have made a political miscalculation as serious as that which conservatives did with Social Security. For 30 years, they have tried to batter down the doors and dismantle Prop. 13, or modify it. Their efforts, frankly, were as doomed as the efforts to change Social Security, because it was considered part of the basic social fabric of California after it passed. All you have to do is look at the poll numbers showing 70% support for the measure today to see that. Some may not like those numbers, but they should understand them rather than just fight against them.

I think Prop. 13 could be modified or improved. But rather than meet supporters of Prop. 13 halfway, its opponents have often taken the Brezhnev approach to political science. The late Soviet leader Leonid Brezhnev was once asked about the future of Europe, and he told western leaders, "What's ours is ours and what's yours is negotiable." Well, with Prop. 13 the message was, "Let's dismantle Prop. 13, because it's destroying the social egalitarianism of California." But what are you going to give the supporters of Prop. 13 today? They represent 70% of the people. You have to give them something as part of a political compromise or else you're not going to get anything.

Instead, in 1990, opponents of Prop. 13 dismantled the Gann spending limit, passed in 1979 by Paul Gann's group, which restricted growth in state government to population and inflation. For growth beyond that it required a vote of the people. It worked to contain the California state budget in the 1980s. We didn't have great fiscal crises in California in the 1980s, except for the recession year of 1983. In general it was a period of relative calm. After the Gann limit was removed in 1990, the state budget went up.

There is much doleful talk about the increases in pressure on state and local governments because of Prop. 13. Many of those problems are real, but let's look at the big picture first. Between 1978 and 2003, the first 25 years of Prop. 13, state school district revenue per student, adjusted for inflation and population increases, went up 30%. The schools may be hurting, but in part it's because there are more administrative personnel and fewer teachers in the classroom than there used to be. But revenue is up overall by 30% in real terms. During the same 25-year-period, state government revenue increased 25% after inflation and population. City governments, which were the governments that were supposedly decimated by Prop. 13, went up 20%.

Now, what's happened since 2003, the year of this decade's first budget crisis? The state budget was $77 billion in 2003. It's now over $100 billion, an increase of 37%. Inflation in those five years has been 15%, population growth you add another 6%, that would lead one to predict a 21% growth rate to keep up with inflation and population growth. But the budget is up 37%.

Supporters of Prop. 13 look at that and say, "Wouldn't it make sense to perhaps contain the state budget deficit that is growing beyond our means of paying for it? Wouldn't a simple way of doing that have been to keep the Gann limit? If spending had to grow beyond that, the people would have to vote on it and that would give a greater legitimacy to the programs so approved."

Sadly, I suspect that kind of grand political compromise is not in the cards. We will continue to remain two camps—those who blindly support Prop. 13 and those who blindly are antagonistic towards it.

I'll conclude on a personal note. Proposition 13 really did mean security for a lot of people. It enabled my mother to stay in her house for the last 30 years, and she died only two weeks ago. She wanted to be at this conference because she felt Prop. 13 was very much an expression of *both* American self-reliance and security. Just as much as you think Social Security is part of the fabric of American security for a lot of people and part of our social safety net, Prop. 13 is just as much a symbol of security for those people. Without it I do think some people would have been forced out of their homes in the late 1970s. The alternative proposed by the legislature, Proposition 8, was viewed as a failed attempt by politicians to recover their credibility. But that credibility was destroyed when State Treasurer, Jesse Unruh, of all people, admitted the state was sitting on a $6 billion surplus. When government failed in California in the mid-1970s, it was different than when the national government failed in the early 1930s. But you were still going to get a populist reaction. Proposition 13 qualified for the ballot by virtue of a record 1.2 million signatures of registered voters—700,000 more than was necessary.

After it passed, Assembly Republican leader Paul Priolo changed his tune, as did then-Governor Jerry Brown. They both agreed the people had spoken. As Priolo said, "This means public officials will have to go to work."

Now, populism has a bad taint in American politics. It's associated with demagoguery and high emotions. But populism properly understood is also an authentic expression of grassroots sentiment. That is what the drive for Social Security was all about.

That's also was what the drive for Proposition 13 was about.

Chapter 3

Proposition 13 Fever: How California's Tax Limitation Spread

Isaac William Martin[1]

On June 6, 1978, California voters approved Proposition 13, a constitutional amendment that cut local property taxes, limited the future growth of property tax revenues, converted the property tax base from market value to acquisition value, and restricted the ability of state and local governments to raise other taxes. Observers at the time saw it as a watershed of national significance. They argued that it was inspiring voters in other states to demand tax limitation laws of their own (Boeth, Lubenow, Kasindorf, and Thomas 1978; Friedman 1978). The nation was said to be in the grip of "Proposition 13 fever" (Kuttner 1980).

If these contemporaries were right about Proposition 13 fever, then much of what we think we know about the economic and fiscal impacts of Proposition 13 may be wrong. Economists and scholars of public administration have found, e.g., that Proposition 13 constrained the growth of government budgets, changed how local governments raise money (Reid 1988; Shires 1999), reduced the quality of local government services (Figlio and Rueben 2001; McGuire and Rueben 1997), and constrained the mobility of homeowners (O'Sullivan, Sexton, and Sheffrin 1995; Wasi and White 2005). But our best estimates of these impacts

---

[1] William Martin Isaac, Department of Sociology, University of California, San Diego.

come from studies that compare California to other states, on the assumption that those states approximate what California would have been like without Proposition 13, so that it is reasonable to treat the comparison as something like an experiment (Campbell and Stanley 1963; King, Keohane, and Verba 1994). If the impact of Proposition 13 spilled over state borders then this research strategy will tend to underestimate the impact of Proposition 13 for two reasons. First, it ignores the impact on other states. And second, spillover contaminates the quasi-experimental comparison, leading the comparison states to look more like post-Proposition-13 California than they would otherwise—and thereby leading us to infer that Proposition 13 made less of a difference than it actually did (Lieberson 1985).

Did the impact of Proposition 13 spill over state borders? The answer is not immediately obvious. Howard Jarvis, one of the authors of the amendment, called it the "shot heard round the nation" and took credit for inspiring subsequent tax cuts in other states (Jarvis and Pack 1979). But Jarvis was notorious for exaggerating his own importance. Opponents of Proposition 13, by contrast, have sometimes tried to make themselves appear successful by minimizing Jarvis's accomplishments (Osborne 1979), and at other times have played up the national impact of Proposition 13 in order to demonstrate the urgency of repealing it (Schrag 1998).

This chapter weighs the evidence, and concludes that Proposition 13 fever was more than a mere metaphor. Both statistical analysis of the available data and interpretive analysis of the historical record show that Proposition 13 did indeed spread via a process of social contagion. One implication of this finding is that Proposition 13 may have had considerably greater impact, for good or ill, than most economists and policy analysts have realized. Another implication is that California voters may have a special responsibility to make good policy. At least sometimes, we make policy not just for California, but for the nation.

Policy Diffusion and Proposition 13 Fever

"Proposition 13 fever" is an example of what political scientists have called *policy diffusion*, or the spread of a policy idea from one jurisdiction to another (Berry and Berry 2007; Karch 2007a; Walker 1969). Policy diffusion is different from mere proliferation. To speak of diffusion is to imply that the actions of policymakers in one jurisdiction have a causal impact on the actions of policymakers in another.

There are reasons to think that policy diffusion is common. Legislators must ordinarily make decisions rapidly in the face of considerable uncertainty about the consequences of those decisions. Given the natural limits on human information processing capacity, they lean heavily on simple decision-making heuristics, and one of the simplest is to imitate a salient policy (Karch 2007a). This quick and dirty (or "fast and frugal" [see Gigerenzer et al. 1999]) decision-making strategy may be particularly important for state policymakers, who do not have the same staff support or information-gathering infrstructure that federal policymakers possess. Policy borrowing may also be particularly easy for state policymakers, since state politics is an institutional domain characterized by two key social conditions for diffusion (see DiMaggio and Powell 1983; Strang and Meyer 1993). First, there are a large number of other states that are culturally defined as analogous, and therefore as legitimate candidates for emulation. Second, there is substantial organizational infrastructure designed specifically to facilitate information-sharing about "best practices," ranging from professional organizations such as the National Conference of State Legislatures, to multistate lobbying organizations, to informal activist networks that make it a point to propagate the policies they prefer (see, e.g., Martin 2001).[2]

Despite the fact that policy diffusion is probably pervasive, it is difficult to establish with certainty in any particular instance that diffusion has taken place. The central problem is the implied causal claim: it is not enough to show that a policy proliferated, but it must also be shown that latecomers adopted the policy in part *because* earlier adopters already did so. The social scientist's usual tools for causal inference are ill suited to this problem. Experiments are usually impossible in policy settings, and always impossible when the research concerns the past. The usual remedy in observational studies—a comparative or "quasi-experimental" research design—is also difficult to implement in the presence of diffusion, because quasi-experimental designs assume that cases are causally independent of one another (King, Keohane, and Verba 1994; Lieberson 1985). It is possible to model diffusion statistically with time-series cross-section data, provided one is willing to impose strong assumptions about the functional form of the interdependence among cases. The best recent work makes use of event-history modeling techniques (Berry and Berry 2007; Strang and Soule 1998; Strang and Tuma 1993). But even in the best case, such quantitative methods are usually not adequate to adjudicate definitively among different causal hypotheses, and they are best supplemented by qualitative data that permits the analyst to trace a policy idea through successive stages of the diffusion process (Karch 2007a; Karch 2007b).

Quantitative Evidence for the Spread of Tax Limitation

In the case of Proposition 13, the record of tax limitation in other states suggests that it is at least plausible to speak of diffusion. Figure 1 illustrates the cumula-

---

[2] In light of this argument, it may come as something of a surprise that political science has devoted comparatively little attention to the study of social diffusion. Everett Rogers's (1995) exhaustive review of diffusion research in the social sciences, e.g., finds 1,454 studies in sociology (including rural sociology and medical sociology), 245 in economics (including agricultural economics), 141 in anthropology, and 129 in political science (including public administration), along with hundreds of others in professional and interdisciplinary fields (Rogers 1995: 42-43).

Figure 1. Tax Limitations Spread Rapidly after 1978

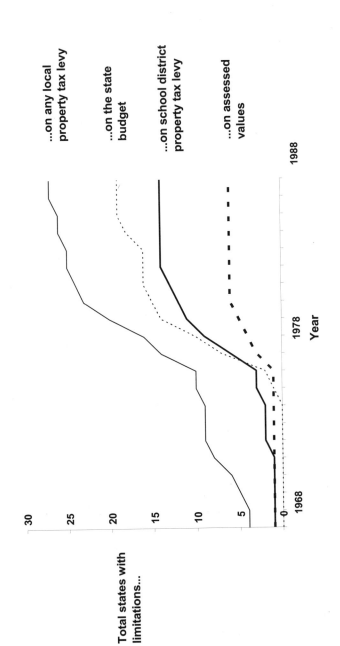

...on any local
property tax levy

...on the state
budget

...on school district
property tax levy

...on assessed
values

Total states with
limitations...

tive number of states that adopted laws similar to Proposition 13. Of course, many different kinds of policies might be called "similar to Proposition 13," because it was a complicated law that packaged together a variety of different provisions that were only loosely related to each other. Rather than impose an arbitrary definition, I have chosen to describe four different kinds of policies that might fit this description, including (1) policies that limit the annual growth of assessed property valuations; (2) policies that effectively limit the annual growth of the total property tax levy of local school districts; (3) policies that effectively limit the annual growth of the total property tax levy of *any* local government, whether school district, county, or municipality; and (4) policies that limit the annual growth of the state budget, whether by limiting the growth of expenditures or revenues.[3] The data were compiled by Mullins and Wallin (2004).

The figure provides our first clue that Proposition 13 diffused to other states. Regardless of which kind of tax limitation policy we consider, the figure shows that it spread more rapidly after 1978. The figure resembles the classic S-shaped diffusion curve that sociologists have found in studies of socially contagious innovations ranging from hybrid seed corn (Ryan and Gross 1943) to pharmaceuticals (Coleman, Katz, and Menzel 1966) to city-manager government (Knoke 1982; for general reviews of the classic diffusion literature, see Rogers 1995 [1962]; Strang and Soule 1998). Moreover, the passage of Proposition 13 in 1978 marks a noticeable point of inflection in all four curves, when the pace of innovation began to increase visibly.

As I have already noted, however, the description of the pattern alone is not conclusive evidence for diffusion. Although a rapid increase in the passage of tax limits followed Proposition 13, it is surely wrong to assume that all of this increase was *because of* Proposition 13. Figure 1 shows, e.g., that a handful of other states had property tax limitations before Proposition 13. It also shows that the pace of tax limitation began to pick up in the early 1970s, even before Proposition 13. We may take these facts as *prima facie* evidence that at least some other states might have found their way to such limitations after 1978 even if Proposition 13 had never passed. And indeed there were several other trends in this period that might have been pushing states toward tax limitation. Rates of home ownership were increasing, making more voters sensitive to property taxes. The cost of public schools was increasing. Average incomes continued to increase, and affluent voters tend to be more conservative.

In order to test whether Proposition 13 really made a difference, I estimated statistical models of the rate of passage before and after Proposition 13 in all states outside of California, controlling for several other factors that might have

---

[3] For my present analytical purposes, an effective limit on the growth of the property tax levy may take the form of an explicit limit on the total levy, or it may arise implicitly from the combination of a limitation on the tax rate combined with a limitation on the growth of assessed valuation. See Joyce and Mullins (1991), Preston and Ichniowski (1991).

affected the passage of tax limits—including the home ownership rate, the black population share, the urban population share, total state personal income per capita, union density, conservative opinion, state and local government spending on education as a percentage of total state personal income, state and local property tax revenues as a percentage of total state personal income, the availability of the ballot initiative, and the number of legislative houses under Republican control.[4] Table 1 reports the annual rate of passage—i.e., the annual probability that a state would pass such a law—and the adjusted rate of passage after controlling for these independent variables. The latter is the annual probability of passage predicted from an event history model by holding all other independent variables constant at their average values (the mean values for continuous variables, and the modal values for categorical variables). The data include annual observations for all states other than California and cover the period from 1965 to 1990. It was not possible to estimate an event-history model of limitations on the growth of assessed values, because the before-and-after variable perfectly predicted the absence of such laws: there was not a single one passed between 1965 and the passage of Proposition 13.

The results reported in Table 1 show clearly that the passage of policies similar to Proposition 13 accelerated after 1978. This is true regardless of what precise variety of tax limitation we consider, and it is true regardless of whether we consider raw rates of passage, or adjust for trends in other variables described above. To grasp the magnitude of the acceleration, we can multiply the annual rate by 49 to express it as the number of states outside of California that might be expected to enact tax limits in a given time period. All else being equal, the before-and-after comparison implies that Proposition 13 increased the rate of school district property tax levy limits from one state every hundred years to one every two years. It increased the rate of local levy limits in general from one state every ten years to two states per year.

Of course, a dichotomous "before-and-after" measure is a crude way to measure the impact of Proposition 13. The measured coefficient of this variable might be a spurious proxy for the influence of *any* unmeasured variable that increased over time. One way to determine whether Proposition 13 really was a unique turning point is to compare 1978 to another arbitrarily chosen year. Was 1978 truly special, or might we just as well have concluded that there was a turning point if we compared the rate of passage before and after 1970, say, or

---

[4] These event history models took the logistic functional form P (passing a tax limit) $= \exp(\alpha+\beta x+\gamma z)/(1+\exp[\alpha+\beta x+\gamma z])$, where α is a constant term, β is a column vector of coefficients, γ is a scalar coefficient, z is a dichotomous variable equal to zero for observations prior to 1978 and equal to one for observations dated 1978 and thereafter, and x is a row vector including all of the independent variables described above. The unit of observation is the state-year, and states are dropped from the data (or "right-censored") after the passage of a tax limit, so the number of observations differs across models (N=1,063 for the analysis of school levy limits, N=882 for the analysis of all levy limits, and N=1,062 for the analysis of state budget limits). Sources of the variables are described in the appendix.

Table 1. Proposition 13 Increased the Rate at which other States Passed Tax Limitation Laws

	Unadjusted rate of passage		Adjusted rate of passage	
	Before Prop. 13	**After Prop. 13**	**Before Prop. 13**	**After Prop. 13**
Any limit on growth of assessed values	0	.007	N/A	N/A
Limit on school district property tax levy[a]	.003	.02	.0002	.008
Limit on any local property tax levy	.01	.04	.002	.04
Limit on growth of state budget	.002	.04	.001	.02

All before-and-after differences are statistically significant ($p<.05$).

"Adjusted rate of passage" is calculated for an average state from an event history model that controls for all of the following variables (see Appendix for sources): the home ownership rate, black population share, urban populaton share, total state personal income per capita, union density, conservative opinion, state and local government spending on education as a percentage of total state personal income, state and local property tax revenues as a percentage of total state personal income, the availability of the ballot initiative, and the number of legislative houses under Republican control.

All event history models fit the data significantly better than a null model ($p<.01$) according to likelihood-ratio chi-squared tests.

[a] Model includes an additional control variable for the presence of a court-ordered school finance equalization, coded from Manwaring and Sheffrin (Manwaring and Sheffrin 1997).

1986? To answer this question, I estimated a series of event history models identical to those reported in Table 1, but specifying each year in turn as a turning point (represented in the regression analysis by a dichotomous "before-and-after" variable). Figure 2 illustrates the results. The horizontal axis represents

Figure 2. Proposition 13 is the Turning Point That Fits the Data Best

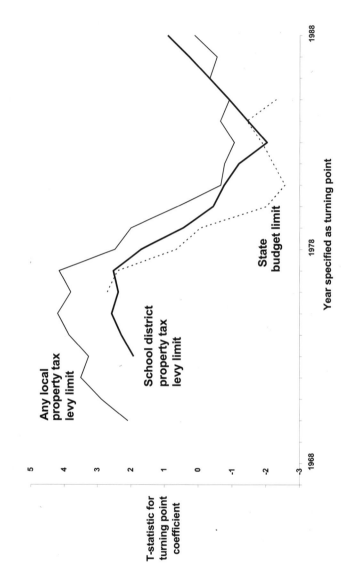

the year that was specified as a turning point, and the vertical axis is a standard measure of how well the coefficient for that turning point fits the data.[5] The figure shows that the models that fit best were those that specified a turning point some time in the period from 1976 to 1978. The turning point seems to fall in this window regardless of which variety of tax limitation policy we consider. This finding does not rule out the possibility that some other event in this period might have made the difference, but it should increase our confidence that there really was a turning point around the time of Proposition 13.

Qualitative Evidence of Diffusion

The statistical evidence is consistent with the spread of Proposition 13 fever, and it rules out some other explanations for the spread of property tax limits, but it does not clinch the case that Proposition 13 was the vector of contagion. If it is true that Proposition 13 caused this wave of tax limits, then we should find evidence in the qualitative record that Proposition 13 changed minds. We should find traces of the contagion not just in observers' generalizations about "Proposition 13 fever," but also in the private documents of politicians and activists, where they communicated policy ideas to each other outside of the public eye.

That is indeed what we find. Because space is limited I will offer only a brief illustrative case study of Michigan. The case is chosen in part because it is distant from California, to illustrate why the event history analysis treated the diffusion of Proposition 13 as a national rather than a regional process (cf. Berry and Berry 2007). This was a truly national diffusion process, not confined to states connected by direct geographic proximity or tax competition or any other form of frequent exchange (see Karch 2007a; Strang and Meyer 1993). The case is also chosen to illustrate two different pathways by which the passage of this tax limit in California affected political decision-making in other states.

The First Pathway: Activist Networks

One way that Proposition 13 fever spread was through loosely connected networks of conservative activists. The example of Proposition 13 led conservative activists in other states to embrace the cause of property tax limitation for the first time, because they saw it as a winning issue.

This was a genuine transformation in the grassroots right. Before 1978, conservative taxpayer activists saw limits on the growth of state spending and limits on the growth of the local property tax as fundamentally different kinds of policy. Indeed, they were perceived to be in conflict: if local property tax relief

---

[5] Specifically, it is the t-statistic calculated from the ratio of the coefficient and the standard error. Values greater than approximately 1.96 indicate that the difference between "before" and "after" is statistically significant at the conventional .05 level.

came at a cost in state spending, it was rejected as unconservative. When Ronald Reagan was governor of California, for example, he had recruited a "kitchen cabinet" of conservative activists to launch an unsuccessful initiative campaign for a limit on the growth of the state budget (Burbank 1993/94), but he opposed several local property tax limitation initiatives that resembled Proposition 13 (Turpin 1972). In Michigan, conservative activists who had ties to Reagan's kitchen cabinet founded a group called Taxpayers United to press for a limit on the state budget, and twice circulated initiatives to limit state taxation while ignoring the local property tax.

After Proposition 13, these conservative activists warmed to property tax limits. The activist Lew Uhler, who had helped to draft Governor Reagan's unsuccessful tax limit initiative in 1973, wrote to the leadership of Taxpayers United in 1978 to tell them that they should get on the Proposition 13 bandwagon. "My cumulative experience has led me to revise the tax limitation model, retitling it 'Property Tax and State Tax Limitation Amendment,' and placing the property tax reduction and limitation sections right up front," he wrote. The point of this, he wrote, was to "ride the political momentum occasioned by the property tax revolt which grips Michigan, California, and many other states."[6] They took his advice, and began circulating a property tax limitation initiative called the Headlee Amendment.

The conservative networks that assisted in the spread of Proposition 13 did not necessarily predate the amendment. Another Michigan conservative activist named Robert Tisch who at first knew Jarvis only through the news media wrote his own tax limitation initiative explicitly modeled on Proposition 13 in the spring of 1978, before Proposition 13 had passed in California. He contacted Jarvis and forged a close connection in the course of his petition drive. Jarvis consulted with him on strategy and flew to Michigan to campaign for the Tisch Amendment (Aamoth 1978; Detroit News 1978).

The Second Pathway: Elected Officials

A second way that the fever spread was by providing elected officials with a salient policy solution for a pressing problem. Rising property taxes—occasioned by the combination of rising home prices and improvements in assessment techniques—were widely perceived as a political crisis. After Proposition 13, politicians, including liberals and moderates, decided that Proposition 13 represented a viable solution to the crisis.

The moderate Republican governor of Michigan provides a clear example. In 1976, Governor William Milliken had sided with the state teacher's union

---

[6] Lewis K. Uhler to James Barrett, January 17, 1977, and Lewis K. Uhler to Richard H. Headlee, February 2, 1977, both in Richard H. Headlee Papers, 1976-1992, "General correspondence—1977" folder, Bentley Historical Library, University of Michigan.

against the tax limitation initiative circulated by Taxpayers United.[7] But a week after Proposition 13 passed, one of his big campaign contributors wrote to tell him it was time to change his position: "I am firmly convinced that a strong position in support of [property tax limitation] is the *only* way that you will be elected to another term as governor. . . . Secondly, if [a] reasonable tax limitation proposal . . . is not enacted, Michigan will be faced with an extreme cutback in tax revenues, such as California's Proposition 13."[8]

The threat was plausible because Tisch was, in fact, circulating a more extreme property tax limitation initiative at the time. Milliken decided to take his contributor's advice. He broke with the teachers and—like much of the rest of the Michigan political establishment—embraced the Headlee Amendment in order to head off the alternative. Michigan voters approved the Headlee Amendment and rejected the Tisch Amendment that fall (Kuttner 1980).

In summary, this qualitative evidence shows that policymakers and activists changed their positions on tax limitation after Proposition 13; that they attributed their changes of heart to Proposition 13; that they described their new preferred policies with reference to the passage of Proposition 13 in California; and that their new Proposition-13-like policy proposals often succeeded where previous efforts to cut or limit taxes had failed. Michigan is only a single example, but published case studies of other states including Massachusetts and New York confirm these generalizations (see Martin 2008: chapter 5). In combination with the statistical evidence presented above, these qualitative case studies are strong evidence that Proposition 13 really did cause the increase in the passage of tax limitations that we observe after 1978.

Implications for Scholars and Policymakers

The chapter has presented evidence that Proposition 13 *did* spread something like a fever. California was contagious. Activists saw it as a model that they could emulate to achieve some of their ends. Policymakers likewise saw it as a policy model that they could use.

This finding implies that much of the best scholarship on the economic or fiscal impacts of Proposition 13 probably understates those impacts, because it considers only impacts of property tax limitation in California. Proposition 13 spilled over from California into other states. It spilled over from the property tax into other policies. And scholars have even begun to accumulate evidence that it spilled over from the state arena into federal fiscal policy as well. Proposi-

---

[7] Hugh McDiarmid, "MEA Takes Full Credit for Defeat of Spending Limit," *Detroit Free Press*, Nov. 4, 1976, n.p., Richard H. Headlee Papers, 1976-1992, "General correspondence—1976" folder, Bentley Historical Library, University of Michigan.

[8] John A. Rapanos to William G. Milliken, June 12, 1978, Box 365, Folder 5, Governor William G. Milliken. Papers, 1969-1982, Executive Office, Communications Division, RG 88-269, State Archives of Michigan.

tion 13 was a pivotal moment that changed how Congress perceived public opinion on taxes and government spending in general. Recent monographs by political sociologists, e.g., present evidence that Proposition 13 shaped congressional debates over federal income tax policy and welfare reform (Prasad 2006; Steensland 2008).

These findings also tell us something about what is at stake today when Californians debate whether and how to reform Proposition 13 and what to do about our system of state and local budgeting in general. Californians like to flatter ourselves that we are trend setters. The case of Proposition 13 shows that at least sometimes we really are. A less flattering way to put the point is that when we sneeze, other states can catch cold.

Of course not every policy that California voters approve is as infectious as Proposition 13. It is beyond the scope of this paper to present a systematic comparative analysis of why some policies diffuse more readily than others. But one reason why Proposition 13 in particular drew so much attention was probably that this was not the policy that outside observers expected from California, which before 1978 was widely stereotyped as a liberal, big-government state (see Schrag 1998). Proposition 13 stood out against this background stereotype as particularly surprising news—and it was therefore assumed to express a major shift in the preferences of the voting public, despite plenty of evidence that those preferences were pretty much the same as before (see Sears and Citrin 1985). The result was a classic self-fulfilling prophecy (Merton 1968 [1949]): Proposition 13 was a bellwether of change because politicians *thought* it was a bellwether of change and changed their behavior accordingly.

Could it happen again? The intervening 30 years have surely changed the stereotype of California held by policymakers in other states. We are now widely known for our unwillingness to pay taxes, and for our chronic budget deficit. Few would be surprised today if California voters approved another tax limitation; it is easier to imagine the national headlines that would result if California voters approved an initiative to undo the limitations of Proposition 13 and increase taxes. Such reforms to Proposition 13 do not seem to be in the immediate offing. But when they come, they too may prove to be catching.

Appendix: Data Sources and Estimation Results from Event History Regression Models

Variable [range]	Sources and notes	Logit coefficient (standard error)		
		School levy limit	Any levy limit	State budget limit
Home owners [44% to 74% of households]	U.S. Bureau of the Census (2002a). Values for intercensal years interpolated linearly.	.24 (.10)	.02 (.06)	.07 (.08)
African Americans [0% to 39% of pop.]	National Cancer Institute (2006). Values for 1965-1967 interpolated linearly.	.01 (.03)	.04 (.03)	.03 (.04)
Urban population share [32% to 89% of pop.]	U.S. Bureau of the Census (2002b). Values for intercensal years interpolated linearly.	.06 (.03)	.03 (.02)	.04 (.03)
Personal income per capita, constant $000s [5.4 to 21.2]	Calculated from U.S. Bureau of Economic Analysis (2002) and National Cancer Institute (2002).	-.46 (.26)	-.27 (.18)	-.03 (.21)
Union membership [4% to 43% of labor force]	Hirsch et al. (2001, 2007).	.02 (.05)	.01 (.04)	.04 (.07)
Conservatives [28% to 44% of survey respondents]	Erikson et al. (1993). Measured by aggregating samples over 1976 to 1988, extrapolated as time-invariant.	-.24 (.16)	-.37 (.13)	-.04 (.21)
State and local education spending [3.3% to 12.6% of personal income]	Calculated from U.S. Bureau of the Census, series GF (various) and U.S. Bureau of Economic Analysis (2002).	.52 (.31)	.70 (.24)	.28 (.33)

State and local property tax revenue [1.0% to 10.9% of personal income]	Calculated from U.S. Bureau of the Census, series GF (various) and U.S. Bureau of Economic Analysis (2002).	-.50 (.33)	-.58 (.23)	-.09 (.35)
Court-ordered school finance equalization? [1=yes, 0=no]	Calculated from Manwaring and Sheffrin (1997)	-.47 (.91)	...	...
Ballot initiative? [1=yes, 0=no]	Council of State Legislatures (various).	1.47 (.82)	1.16 (.67)	1.21 (.78)
Republican-controlled legislative houses [0 to 2]	U.S. Bureau of the Census (various years), Statistical Abstract.	-.68 (.63)	.62 (.33)	-.23 (.59)
After Proposition 13? [1=yes, 0=no]	Coded yes for 1978 or later.	3.60 (1.42)	3.09 (.74)	2.71 (1.13)
Constant term		-16.38 (4.87)	3.03 (5.81)	-14.75 (6.60)

References

Aamoth, Nila. 1978. "Jousting Tax Windmills: Ordinary Citizens Are Carrying Banners for Lower Taxes; Quixotic or Chaotic?" *Grand Rapids Photo Reporter*, June 20, p. 1.

Berry, Frances Stokes, and William D. Berry. 2007. "Innovation and Diffusion Models in Policy Research." In *Theories of the Policy Process*, ed. P. A. Sabatier. Boulder: Westview Press, 223-60.

Boeth, Richard, Gerald C. Lubenow, Martin Kasindorf, and Rich Thomas. 1978. "The Big Tax Revolt." *Newsweek*, June 19, pp. 20-30.

Burbank, Garin. 1993/94. "Governor Reagan's Only Defeat: The Proposition 1 Campaign in 1973." *California History* 72:360-73.

Campbell, Donald T., and Julian Stanley. 1963. *Experimental and Quasi-Experimental Designs for Research*. New York: Houghton Mifflin.

Coleman, James S., Elihu Katz, and Herbert Menzel. 1966. *Medical Innovation: A Diffusion Study*. New York: Bobbs-Merrill Co.

Council of State Legislatures. Various years. *The Book of the States*. Lexington, Kentucky: Council of State Legislatures.

Detroit News. 1978. "Tax Limit Drive Gets a Plug from Jarvis." *Detroit News*, July 26.

DiMaggio, Paul J., and Walter W. Powell. 1983. "The Iron Cage Revisited: Institutional Isomorphism and Collective Rationality in Organizational Fields." *American Sociological Review* 48:147-60.

Erikson, Robert S., Gerald C. Wright, and John P. McIver. 1993. *Statehouse Democracy: Public Opinion and Policy in the American States*. New York: Cambridge University Press.

Figlio, David N., and Kim S. Rueben. 2001. "Tax Limits and the Qualifications of New Teachers." *Journal of Public Economics* 80:49-71.

Friedman, Milton. 1978. "The Message from California." *Newsweek*, June 19, p. 24.

Gigerenzer, Gerd, Peter M. Todd, and the ABC Research Group. 1999. *Simple Heuristics That Make Us Smart*. New York: Oxford University Press.

Hirsch, Barry T., David A. Macpherson, and Wayne G. Vroman. 2001. "Estimates of Union Density by State." *Monthly Labor Review* 124 (7): 51-55.

Hirsch, Barry T., David A. Macpherson, and Wayne G. Vroman. 2007. "State Union Membership Density, 1964-2007." Data file available as of November 19, 2008 from http://www.trinity.edu/bhirsch/StateUnionMembershipDensity 1964-2002.xls.

Jarvis, Howard, and Robert Pack. 1979. *I'm Mad as Hell*. New York: Times Books.

Joyce, Philip G., and Daniel R. Mullins. 1991. "The Changing Fiscal Structure of the State and Local Public Sector: The Impact of Tax and Expenditure Limitations." *Public Administration Review* 51:240-53.

Karch, Andrew. 2007a. *Democratic Laboratories: Policy Diffusion among the American States*. Ann Arbor: University of Michigan Press.

————. 2007b. "Emerging Issues and Future Directions in State Policy Diffusion Research." *State Politics and Policy Quarterly* 7:54-80.

King, Gary, Robert O. Keohane, and Sidney Verba. 1994. *Designing Social Inquiry*. Princeton: Princeton University Press.

Knoke, David. 1982. "The Spread of Municipal Reform: Temporal, Spatial, and Social Dynamics." *American Journal of Sociology* 87:1314-39.

Kuttner, Robert. 1980. *The Revolt of the Haves: Tax Rebellions and Hard Times.* New York: Simon and Schuster.

Lieberson, Stanley. 1985. *Making It Count: The Improvement of Social Research and Theory*. Berkeley and Los Angeles: University of California Press.

Manwaring, Robert, and Steven M. Sheffrin. 1997. "Litigation, School Finance Reform, and Aggregate Educational Spending." *International Tax and Public Finance* 4:107-27.

Martin, Isaac William. 2001. "Dawn of the Living Wage: The Diffusion of a Redistributive Municipal Policy." *Urban Affairs Review* 36:470-96.

Martin, Isaac William. 2008. *The Permanent Tax Revolt: How the Property Tax Transformed American Politics*. Stanford: Stanford University Press.

McGuire, Therese J., and Kim Rueben. 1997. "Tax and Bond Referenda in California and Illinois: Observations on Local Governments Operating under State-Imposed Restraints." *Proceedings of the National Tax Association* 89: 169-81.

Merton, Robert K. 1968 [1949]. *Social Theory and Social Structure*. New York: The Free Press.

Mullins, Daniel R., and Bruce A. Wallin. 2004. "Tax and Expenditure Limitations: Introduction and Overview." *Public Budgeting and Finance* 24:2-15.

National Cancer Institute. 2002. SEER Population Files. Data available as of November 19, 2008 from http://seer.cancer.gov/popdata/download.html.

O'Sullivan, Arthur, Terri A. Sexton, and Steven M. Sheffrin. 1995. *Property Taxes and Tax Revolts: The Legacy of Proposition 13*. Cambridge, England: Cambridge University Press.

Osborne, David. 1979. "Renegade Tax Reform: Turning Prop. 13 on its Head." *SR*, May 12, pp. 20-23.

Prasad, Monica. 2006. *The Politics of Free Markets: The Rise of Neoliberal Economic Policies in Britain, France, Germany, and the United States*. Chicago: University of Chicago Press.

Preston, Anne E., and Casey Ichniowski. 1991. "A National Perspective on the Nature and Effects of the Local Property Tax Revolt, 1976-1986." *National Tax Journal* 44:123-45.

Reid, Gary J. 1988. "How Cities in California Have Responded to Fiscal Pressures Since Proposition 13." *Public Budgeting and Finance* 8:20-37.

Rogers, Everett M. 1995 [1962]. *Diffusion of Innovations*. New York: Free Press.

Ryan, Bryce, and Neal C. Gross. 1943. "The Diffusion of Hybrid Seed Corn in Two Iowa Communities." *Rural Sociology* 8:15-24.

Schrag, Peter. 1998. *Paradise Lost: California's Experience, America's Future*. Berkeley: University of California.

Sears, David O., and Jack Citrin. 1985. *Tax Revolt: Something for Nothing in California.* Cambridge, Mass.: Harvard University Press.

Shires, Michael A. 1999. *Patterns in California Government Revenues since Proposition 13.* San Francisco: Public Policy Institute of California.

Steensland, Brian. 2008. *The Failed Welfare Revolution: America's Struggle over Guaranteed Income Policy.* Princeton: Princeton University Press.

Strang, David, and John Meyer. 1993. "Institutional Conditions for Diffusion." *Theory and Society* 22:487-511.

Strang, David, and Sarah A. Soule. 1998. "Diffusion in Organizations and Social Movements: From Hybrid Corn to Poison Pills." *Annual Review of Sociology* 24:265-90.

Strang, David, and Nancy Brandon Tuma. 1993. "Spatial and Temporal Heterogeneity in Diffusion." *American Journal of Sociology* 99:614-39.

Turpin, Dick. 1972. "Reagan and Watson Clash over Prop. 14 at Realtors' Meeting." *Los Angeles Times*, E14.

U.S. Bureau of the Census. 2002. "Historical Census of Housing Tables: Homeownership," downloaded March 26, 2002 from http://www.census.gov/hhes/www/housing/census/historic/owner.html.

U.S. Bureau of the Census. 2002. "Urban and Rural Population: 1900 to 1990," retrieved March 26, 2002 from http://www.census.gov/population/censusdata/urpop0090.txt.

U.S. Bureau of the Census. Various years. *Governmental Finances* (series GF). Washington, D.C.: U.S. Bureau of the Census.

U.S. Bureau of the Census. Various years. *Statistical Abstract of the United States.* Washington, D.C.: U.S. Bureau of the Census.

U.S. Bureau of Economic Analysis. 2002. "Regional Accounts Data," retrieved March 27, 2002 from http://www.bea.doc.gov/bea/regional/spi/.

Walker, Jack L. 1969. "The Diffusion of Innovations among the American States." *American Political Science Review* 63:880-99.

Wasi, Nada, and Michelle J. White. 2005. "Property Tax Limitations and Mobility: Lock-In Effects of California's Proposition 13." *Brookings-Wharton Papers on Urban Affairs* 2005: 59-88.

Chapter 4

Coping through California's Budget Crises in Light of Proposition 13 and California's Fiscal Constitution

David Gamage[1]

When Proposition 13 passed in 1978, many commentators predicted disaster for California's state and local finances. Now, 30 years later, California is experiencing severe fiscal instability and a round of budget crises that has been worse than in the other states.

It would be wrong to blame Proposition 13 for all of California's financial woes. Nevertheless, Proposition 13 is both an important component and a powerful symbol of California's flawed fiscal constitution.

The phrase "fiscal constitution" refers to the rules and processes whereby states and localities make decisions regarding taxes and spending. Hence, California's fiscal constitution consists of its initiative process in addition to its legislative budgeting process.

Many commentators have critiqued California's fiscal constitution from ideological perspectives. From the vantage point of someone who desires higher taxes

---

[1] David Gamage is an assistant professor at the UC Berkeley School of Law.

and spending, the problem lies with the restrictions imposed on raising revenues—such as Proposition 13's limits on property taxes. On the other hand, from the perspective of someone who thinks taxes and spending are too high, the problem may lie with automatic spending programs, overspending during economic upturns, or in a disconnect between legislators' spending preferences and those of the voters.

This chapter attempts to navigate between these ideological perspectives to seek nonpartisan solutions to California's repeated budget crises. Regardless of one's preferences for the levels of taxes and spending, state and local finances need to be managed in the face of political disagreement and changing economic conditions. Although liberals might view California as having a revenue problem, and conservatives a spending problem, the disconnect between current revenues and current expenditures is a problem that all can agree on.

Despite the predictions of some overly enthusiastic commentators, the internet revolution of the 1990s did not eliminate the business cycle. As long as state economies cycle between booms and busts, states will face predictable uncertainty regarding future revenues. We can thus expect budget crises to be a regular feature of California's fiscal landscape in the coming decades. These crises will likely be interspersed with periods of strong economic growth and revenue surpluses. But without dramatic changes to California's fiscal constitution, these growth periods will be only temporary calms between fiscal storms.

This chapter will begin by discussing the relationship between state budget crises and the business cycle, and why California's unique tax structure creates a worse fiscal rollercoaster than in the other states. However, the focus of this chapter is on the manner in which California's fiscal constitution exacerbates its budgetary roller coaster. The chapter will present and analyze a number of alternatives for reforming California's fiscal constitution so as to ameliorate the dynamics currently leading to repeated harmful budget crises.

The Role of the Business Cycle

Perhaps the most important cause of state budget crises is the ordinary working of the business cycle. Unfortunately, the economic causes of the business cycle are not fully understood. Many of the most prominent theories involve elements of psychology in addition to or in place of neo-classical economic reasoning. It seems likely that economic actors become overly optimistic about future prospects during upturns, leading to excess investment and inventory buildup, which ultimately creates the need for readjustments and cutbacks during economic downturns.

Whatever the underlying causes of business cycles, there is general recognition that business cycles exist and that they are likely to continue to exist for the foreseeable future. From the perspective of state fiscal management—rather than macro-economic management—the most important features of the business cycle are its implications for taxes and spending programs. During economic downturns, tax revenues plummet just as the demand for many spending programs increase.

The reverse happens during upturns: revenues accumulate while the demand for spending programs decreases.

The shift from an upturn to a downturn can be abrupt, with profound consequences for state budgeting. For instance, California's general fund revenues grew 20% in 2000—the final year of the internet boom—only to fall by 17% in 2002.[2] Liberals and conservatives can argue about whether spending was too high in 2000, or too low in 2002, but it cannot be disputed that the budgets passed assuming a continuation of the economic conditions of the late 1990s proved a poor match for the conditions of the current decade.

With perfect hindsight, it is easy to blame poor budgeting on shortsighted or irresponsible behavior by legislators or by forecasting staffs.[3] But passing blame in this fashion ignores the realities of the forecasting process.[4] Although many experts predicted the end of the tech boom, forecasters had no way of knowing exactly how long the boom would last. Indeed, there was no shortage of commentators proclaiming an end to the business cycle and arguing that the strong growth of the late 1990s would continue for decades.

Even were forecasters able to ignore the most optimistic projections, it is not sufficient to know that a boom will eventually end (or that a bubble will eventually burst). Forecasters need to make predictions on a year-by-year basis. Forecasters sometimes stress the uncertainty of their projections. But disclaimers and other means for conveying uncertainty are notoriously easy to ignore in favor of the hard numbers of the actual projections. Ultimately, state budget processes require hard numbers, and even uncertain numbers have a great deal of influence.

Unless economists or other scholars create new technologies for predicting the future course of state economies and budgets that are vastly superior to the methods we have today, states will continue to experience dramatic revenue swings as their economies cycle between booms and busts. The necessary and painful adjustments that states will need to make at the beginning of each downturn are the primary cause of budget crises.

The Role of California's Tax Base

California relies on income taxation for a greater proportion of its overall revenues than does almost any other state while relying on property taxation much

---

[2] Jon David Vasche and Brad Williams, "Revenue Volatility in California," *State Tax Notes*, Apr. 4, 2005, p. 35.

[3] There is some evidence that state forecasting is slightly biased in a politically motivated fashion, but this bias does not explain inaccurate forecasts of changing economic conditions. Richard T. Boylan, "Political Distortions in State Forecasts," *Public Choice*, Apr. 2008.

[4] *See* National Association of State Budget Officers, "Budgeting Amid Fiscal Uncertainty: Ensuring Budget Stability by Focusing on the Long Run," 2004 (hereinafter *NASBO 2004*).

less than do the other states. Proposition 13 is perhaps the most important cause of California's unique tax structure.[5] Property tax collections in California fell by over 50% following the enactment of Proposition 13 in 1978. Subsequently, the growth of property tax revenues in the 30 years following Proposition 13 has been much slower in California than in the other states while the growth of income tax collections has been considerably faster.[6]

California's tax mix results in significantly greater fiscal volatility, because income tax revenues are amongst the most volatile of the major state funding sources while property tax revenues are among the least volatile. This greater volatility of California's revenue structure has led to California enjoying a larger degree of enhanced fiscal capacity during economic upturns, but has also led to dramatically more severe budget crises during economic downturns.

The defenders of Proposition 13 sometimes draw attention to the fact that Proposition 13 has decreased the volatility of California's property tax revenues. Since Proposition 13 limits the growth of appraised values for the purposes of property tax assessment even when market values are growing rapidly, most homeowners find that over time their appraised values are much lower than the market values of their homes. If market property values later fall—as is currently happening in California—homeowners will not see a reduction in their tax bills unless the market values fall to below the appraised values for property tax assessment. Hence, property tax revenues may continue growing even during periods of housing price decline.

Yet despite Proposition 13's reduction in volatility of California's property tax revenues, this effect is dwarfed by the greater volatility that has resulted from shifting California's tax base away from property taxation and toward income taxation. Even in states without property tax limitations, property taxes remain one of the least volatile sources of state revenue.[7] Moreover, whereas the other major sources of state revenues tend to rise and fall simultaneously, property tax revenues tend to follow their own course. Property tax revenues sometimes rise and fall with the overall state economy—as is currently taking place. But it is not uncommon for property tax revenues to continue rising while the state economy and its other revenue sources are entering a downturn—as occurred in 2001. Due to both the greater stability of property taxes and to their countercyclical tendencies, were California able to increase its use of property taxation, the volatility of the

---

[5] Proposition 13 had three major components: first, it limited ad valorem property taxes to a maximum rate of 1% (with a few exceptions); second, it limited the rate at which the assessed value of property can increase for property tax purposes to 2%, even during periods when the real value of a property is increasing far more rapidly; and third, it imposed a two-thirds super-majority requirement on any legislatively enacted change to state taxes for the purposes of raising revenue.

[6] Public Policy Institute of California, "Fiscal Realities: Budget Tradeoffs in California Government," 2007, p. 26.

[7] J. Fried Giertz, "The Property Tax Bound," *National Tax Journal*, Sept. 2006; Russell S. Sobel and Gary A. Wagner, "Cyclical Variability In State Government Revenue: Can Tax Reform Reduce It?" *State Tax Notes*, Aug. 25, 2003.

state's revenue structure would be greatly reduced and budgetary crises would become both less common and less severe.

Another factor leading to greater fiscal volatility in California and thus to more severe budget crises during downturns is California's relatively high reliance on capital gains taxation. California is one of only seven states that taxes capital gains at the same rates as ordinary income, and California derives a much higher percentage of its overall revenues from capital gains taxation than do most of the other states.[8] Over the last 30 years, capital gains have been five times more volatile than wages and salaries or than consumption. Hence, revenues from capital gains taxation are considerably more volatile than revenues from the taxation of ordinary income or sales taxes.

Some commentators have suggested that California should move away from taxing capital gains and shift toward a less volatile tax base. Yet the most volatile sources of state revenue are also the most progressive sources of state revenue. Hence, switching toward a more stable tax base requires moving toward a regressive tax base—by moving away from taxing capital and/or taxing ordinary income at high marginal rates. Property taxes are unique among the major sources of state revenue in that they are relatively nonvolatile, while taxing capital (at least to some extent) and being capable (at least arguably) of progressivity in their incidence.[9]

If California voters wish to retain the level of progressivity currently embedded in California's tax structure, and do not wish to overturn Proposition 13 and enact significantly higher property taxes, California's revenue structure will continue to exhibit high levels of fiscal volatility. Without major reforms to either California's tax base structure or to the state's fiscal constitution, we should expect repeated budget crises over the coming decades. If current trends continue, these budget crises are likely to become increasingly severe. Californians may end up looking back on their current budget troubles with nostalgia.

The Role of California's Fiscal Constitution

Due to the workings of the business cycle and to long-term trends in the economics of health care and education spending, budget crises will continue to be

---

[8] The other states are Hawaii, Idaho, Iowa, Maine, Minnesota, and North Carolina. David L. Sjoquist and Sally Wallace, "Capital Gains: Its Recent, Varied, and Growing (?) Impact on State Revenues," *State Tax Notes*, Aug. 18, 2003, p. 498.

[9] The extent to which property taxes burden capital as opposed to other sources is controversial, as is the degree to which property taxes can be made progressive. *See* George R. Zodrow, "The Property Tax Incidence Debate and the Mix of State and Local Finance of Local Public Expenditures," *CESifo Economic Studies*, Jan. 2008. Note, however, that property taxes can be made more progressive through the use of circuit breakers and related devices. *See* Karen Lyons, Sarah Farkas, and Nicholas Johnson, "The Property Tax Circuit Breaker: An Introduction and Survey of Current Programs," Report by the Center on Budget and Policy Priorities, March 21, 2007.

a recurring part of California's fiscal landscape.[10] Due to California's choice of a highly volatile (and more progressive) tax base, these crises will almost undoubtedly be more severe in California than in the other states. In light of these challenges, it is of crucial importance for California's political establishment to be able to confront the hard choices presented by budget crises head on. Unfortunately, the structure of California's fiscal constitution stands in the way of proactive solutions to California's budgetary dilemmas.

As in all states, California's political establishment is composed of diverse interest groups who have different preferences for tax and spending policy. Some of these groups would like to see taxes lowered, while other groups would like to see additional revenues raised to fund their desired spending programs. During times of significant budgetary shortfalls, the conflicts between these groups can become particularly salient.

Were the state legislature the sole arbiter of budget policy, and were the legislature not bound by supermajority requirements, responses to budget shortfalls would primarily depend on which mix of interest groups controlled a majority of votes in the legislature. If pro-spending groups controlled a majority, we would expect to see tax hikes. Similarly, we would expect spending cuts if anti-tax interest groups controlled a majority. Or if neither side controlled a sufficiently strong majority, we might expect a compromise policy containing both tax hikes and spending cuts.

Yet California's fiscal constitution differs from this picture in a number of important respects. Not only does it take more than a simple majority of the state legislature to enact budgetary reforms, but the state legislature is far from the only arena in which budgetary policy can be enacted. These factors combine to create an environment in which interest groups often find it far easier to advance their policy preferences through the initiative process than through the legislative process.

Looking first to the legislative process, California's constitution requires a two-thirds majority vote in both chambers to pass a budget or to raise taxes.[11] These supermajority requirements enable a determined minority of the legislature to block any budgetary reform the minority disagrees with. When combined with the governor's veto and other legislative roadblocks, the two-thirds supermajority requirement makes it unlikely that any political party or coalition of interest

---

[10] Education and healthcare spending in the United States has been growing faster than gross domestic product. In particular, healthcare spending jumped to 15% of GDP in 2007, from under 5% of GDP in 1960. If current trends continue, the Congressional Budget Office projects that healthcare spending will grow to over 45% of GDP by 2080. This massive growth of healthcare expenditures threatens to overwhelm the funding power of both the states and the national government, causing programs like Medicaid take over a continually increasing percentage of state budgets. Congressional Budget Office, "The Long Term Budget Outlook," Dec. 2007, pp. 22-24.

[11] The two-thirds super-majority requirement for raising taxes was placed in the state Constitution by Proposition 13 in 1978. The two-thirds super-majority requirement for passing budgets dates back to the Riley-Stewart Amendment enacted in 1933.

groups will have a sufficient majority to enact their desired budgetary reforms in the face of determined opposition.

Exacerbating this problem is California's system of term limits that gives state legislators little incentive to compromise in the short term in order to build longer-term working relationships. There is little that a majority coalition can offer the minority in order to gain the minority's acquiescence in passing a legislative response to a budget crisis.

Were the legislative process the only arena in which interest groups could hope to have their policy goals enacted, these obstacles to majority decision-making might successfully force compromise. With no other option available, the diverse interest groups might be forced to come together to agree on solutions to budget shortfalls. But the legislative process is hardly the only game in town.

California's initiative process gives interest groups a ready alternative to the legislature for achieving their budgetary policy goals. California's voters can constrain and override decisions of the legislature through use of ballot initiatives. Proposition 13 is the most notable example of voters using initiatives to shape California's fiscal constitution, but it is not the only example.

Consider this partial list of the initiatives affecting California's budget that were passed following the adoption of Proposition 13 in 1978:

- In 1979, Proposition 4 created state spending limits, such that annual appropriations are limited based on prior year appropriations and revenues in excess of these limits must be returned.
- In 1982, Propositions 5 and 6 abolished the state's inheritance and gift taxes. Also, Proposition 7 required a partial indexing of the state's income tax.
- In 1986, Proposition 47 required that revenue from motor vehicle license fees be allocated to cities and counties. Also, Proposition 62 required that new local taxes be approved by a two-thirds vote of the governing body and a majority of local voters.
- In 1988, Proposition 98 mandated that 40% of the state's general account budget be dedicated to K-12 education and to community college funding. Also, Proposition 99 added a 25-cent sales tax per pack of cigarettes with the proceeds dedicated to health, education, and recreation.
- In 1990, Proposition 111 relaxed some of the previously adopted appropriation limits.
- In 1993, Proposition 172 raised the state's general sales tax by 0.5% with the revenues dedicated to public safety programs.
- In 1996, Proposition 218 strengthened the voter approval requirements for new local taxes, mandating that two-thirds of voters approve new local non-general taxes.
- In 1998, Proposition 10 increased the tax on cigarettes by 25 cents per pack with the revenues dedicated to childhood development programs.
- In 2002, Proposition 42 required that motor vehicle fuel sales and use tax revenues be dedicated to transportation purposes. Also, Proposition 49 mandated an increase in state funding for after school programs.

- In 2004, Proposition 1A adopted several measures to protect local funding sources. Also, Proposition 58 established a budget reserve fund and placed restrictions on the use of deficit bonds and Proposition 63 levied an additional 1% income tax on taxpayers with incomes in excess of $1 million with the revenues dedicated to mental health services.

As this partial list should make clear, voter initiatives play a very important role in shaping California's budget policy. Even the voter recall of Governor Gray Davis in 2003 can be viewed as part of California's fiscal constitution, as the success of the recall has been viewed as coming at least partially in response to Governor Davis's tripling of California's vehicle license fees.

Admittedly, the need to gather a large number of signatures in order to qualify an initiative for the ballot is a major hurdle in using the initiative process as an alternative to the legislative process. But once an initiative qualifies for the ballot, it only requires a simple majority of voters in order to become law, even when the initiative contains a constitutional amendment. Whereas legislative budgetary reforms require two-thirds votes in both chambers, a budgetary initiative needs only the support of half of the voters plus one. For an interest group coalition whose will is thwarted in the legislature, this dynamic can make the initiative process a very attractive alternative.

Moreover, it is often easier to pass budgetary initiatives than the fifty-percent-plus-one math would suggest. Recent research in political psychology has confirmed that voters find it very difficult to understand budgetary tradeoffs. Voters are far more supportive of tax cuts, or of increased spending on popular programs, when these questions are asked in isolation. When voters are asked to evaluate a budgetary package including both tax cuts and reductions in specific spending programs (or increased funding for spending programs along with specified tax hikes) the voters are far less likely to approve of the measures. Psychologist Jonathan Baron and law professor Edward McCaffery have labeled this voter tendency the "isolation effect." Reviewing the experimental evidence, they conclude that political actors—such as the sponsors of ballot initiatives—can manipulate voter responses by controlling the framing of how budgetary decisions are described.

This political psychology research confirms what many political analysts have been claiming for decades. As many a liberal politician has been heard to joke: voters seem to think there is a budgetary line item called "waste and inefficiency" that can be reduced to pay for tax cuts.

Due to the isolation effect, any tax cut or tax restriction measure that makes it to the ballot is likely to generate significant voter support. Similarly, any ballot measure that increases spending on popular programs is also likely to receive significant voter approval. The opponents of these measures will undoubtedly try to explain the tradeoffs and budgetary implications of reducing revenues or tying up funds, but these opponents will start with a major disadvantage as the sponsors of the ballot initiatives will initially control the framing of the initiatives. Without a massive media campaign to explain the stakes to the voting public, it will be all too easy for voters to approve both the tax cuts and the spending hikes, regardless of the consequences for the state's budget.

California's fiscal constitution is thus characterized by both a supermajority requirement and other restrictions that impede budgetary decision making at the legislative level, and a relatively accessible alternative in the initiative process. This combination gives interest groups little incentive to compromise or to work together on proactive solutions to California's long-term budgetary problems.

What Can Be Done?

Of course, the best way to resolve a budget crisis is for the state legislature to come together to pass some combination of tax hikes and/or spending cuts. If exhortations could suffice, this chapter would end with a call for legislators to rise above their parochial interests in order to reach a long-term budgetary compromise.

Yet the United States' political system was built on a Madisonian understanding that political actors will pursue their own narrow interests and must thus be constrained by institutional structures. This chapter has argued that the failure of California's politicians to responsibly deal with the state's budgetary problems is at least partially the fault of the state's flawed fiscal constitution. As such, it is worth considering potential reforms to California's fiscal constitution. The remainder of this chapter will present and analyze a number of possible reforms.

Greater Use of Rainy Day Funds

Once California's economy recovers, the state will likely enjoy a period of budgetary surpluses before the next downturn and resulting budget crisis. Were California able to save the surplus revenues generated during the upturn in a rainy day fund, this would go a long way toward minimizing the pain during subsequent downturns.

Rainy day funds (or budget stabilization funds) help to ward off budget crises in two ways. First, the revenues saved in a rainy day fund can be used to maintain spending during subsequent downturns without the need to raise taxes. Second, any revenues placed in a rainy day fund during an upturn are thus not available for increased spending or for tax cuts during the upturn. Hence, to the extent revenues are stored in a rainy day fund, they cannot be used to create unsustainable policy changes that will haunt the state in the next budget crisis.

California already has a rainy day fund. Indeed, revenues stored in the state's rainy day fund exceeded 10% of general fund expenditures in both the 1999-2000 and 2005-2006 fiscal years—the final year of the 1990s tech boom and of the mid-decade partial recovery driven by the housing bubble.[12] Recognizing the advantages of rainy day funds, Governor Schwarzenegger has called for mandatory caps

---

[12] California Department of Finance, "Historical Data Budget Expenditures," Jan. 2006, *available at* http://www.dof.ca.gov/Budget/BudgetCharts/chart-b.pdf.

on future spending increases with any excess revenues automatically diverted to the state's rainy day fund.

California would undoubtedly benefit from greater use of rainy day funds. But other states' experiences with proposals for mandatory contributions to rainy day funds do not provide much cause for optimism. Remember that state forecasters—both government employees and their private sector equivalents—tend to be overly optimistic in their future projections during economic upturns. When state coffers are overflowing, large surpluses stored in rainy day funds become a tempting target for any politician who seeks to implement a new spending program or to pass a tax cut. Political actors are generally rewarded for "bringing home the bacon"—passing tax cuts or spending hikes that their constituents desire. Fiscal prudence is seldom rewarded at the ballot box, as the beneficial consequences of this prudence are not felt until many years in the future. California's system of term limits exacerbates this problem by causing legislators to focus even more on the short term.

Nevertheless, it is probably still worth experimenting with different methods for increasing the use of rainy day funds during boom years. Mandatory spending caps seem a poor way to achieve this end, however, as spending caps have generally proven easy to evade and do not apply to unsustainable tax cuts—including spending-like tax expenditures. Ultimately, increased funding for rainy day funds will only occur to the extent there is political support for protecting the rainy day fund revenues. Any mandates or prohibitions passed during bust years will be all too easy to overturn or circumvent if they are not backed up by a sufficient degree of political support.

Consequently, the best mechanism for increasing the use of rainy day funds may be to dedicate all revenues from capital gains taxation to the rainy day fund, making these revenues unavailable for general account spending. As capital gains taxes are by far the most volatile of state funding sources, this approach has the advantage of reinforcing a norm that capital gains revenues should not be used to fund long-term budgetary commitments. To divert capital gains revenues or other rainy day funds to support general account spending, the legislature might then be required to declare the existence of a budget crisis through a supermajority vote (ideally requiring a larger supermajority than needed to pass a budget, perhaps a three-fourths supermajority if the current supermajority requirements for passing a budget are maintained).

Whether capital gains revenues are dedicated to rainy day funds, or whether some other approach is devised to increase the use of rainy day funds, it will be necessary to create a robust political understanding that rainy day funds are only to be used when the state is experiencing a significant economic downturn. Without political support for such a norm, no mandatory rule is likely to be successful.

Amend the Supermajority Requirement for Passing Budgets

Numerous reform commissions have recommended abolishing California's two-thirds supermajority requirement for passing state budgets. As the discussion here has undoubtedly made clear, this chapter supports these recommendations. However, when given the option of ending this requirement by passing Proposition 56 in 2004, voters defeated the proposition by a nearly 2-to-1 margin.[13] At least for now, it seems likely that the supermajority requirement is here to stay.

Perhaps more politically feasible would be to relax the supermajority requirement so as to allow the passage of an emergency budget during downturns with a simple majority vote. A constitutional amendment might be passed such that when the state controller declares a downturn or a budget crisis, and this declaration is ratified by a simple majority in both legislative chambers, the supermajority requirement would be temporarily waived.

Emergency budgets passed without a supermajority vote might be limited so that only temporary tax hikes and/or spending cuts are permitted. At the beginning of each year, both the controller and the legislature could be required to reauthorize the existence of a downturn or budget crisis, with all of the provisions in the emergency budget lasting only as long as this reauthorization continues.

To assuage potential concerns about one party controlling both the legislature and the controller's office and using this control to reauthorize emergency budgets into perpetuity, the approval of these budgets could require an escalating supermajority vote.[14] Whereas a simple majority might suffice to keep the emergency budget in effect for the first couple years, the vote threshold for reauthorizing the budget could be gradually increased in subsequent years until it reached the two-thirds supermajority requirement for authorizing nonemergency budgets.

Determining the political feasibility of a proposal to exempt emergency budgets from the two-thirds supermajority requirement is beyond the scope of this chapter. However, the approach has the advantage of giving the legislature more flexibility in responding to budget crises while still requiring a substantial consensus to change the long-term path of California's budget. By exempting emergency budgets from the supermajority requirement, California could hopefully avoid some of the dynamics that have led to long-delays in passing California's budgets and to the repeated use of gimmicks when budgets are passed during down-turns.

---

[13] Proposition 56 – known as the Budget Accountability Act – would have reduced the super-majority requirement for passing the budget from requiring a 2/3rds majority to requiring a 55% majority. The Proposition would also have made the Governor and Legislators lose salary for every day the budget was delivered late. The measure failed to pass with 2,185,868 (34.3%) votes in favor and 4,183,188 (65.7%) against.

[14] The concept of an escalating super-majority vote is drawn from a proposal by Bruce Ackerman for how the United States Congress should deal with authorizing emergency powers. Bruce Ackerman, "Before the Next Attack: Preserving Civil Liberties in an Age of Terrorism," 2006.

Reform the Initiative Process

California's ballot initiative process was designed so that voters would have a check on unresponsive legislatures. To some extent, this process may be achieving its goals in the fiscal realm. It is certainly plausible that Proposition 13 was passed due to legislative unresponsiveness to voter anger about property taxes. Similar stories could be told about most—if not all—of the other budget-affecting ballot initiatives adopted over the last 30 years.

However, when combined with the two-thirds supermajority rule for the legislature to raise taxes or to pass a budget, the initiative process has moved much of the locus of fiscal policymaking away from the legislature. The overall structure of California's fiscal constitution has thus impeded voter accountability.

California's legislature is currently dominated by Democrats who appear to desire higher taxes and spending. Were the legislative process allowed to proceed unchecked, we might expect this coalition to increase taxes and spending until voters protested by electing more fiscal conservatives. But under the current system, the minority coalition is generally able to block significant budgetary changes, resulting in gridlock and the lack of a clearly accountable party.

In light of these dynamics, a case might be made for disallowing voter initiatives with budgetary consequences. Considering the conclusions from recent political psychology research that voters find it particularly difficult to understand budgetary tradeoffs, fiscal policy is perhaps an area for which the legislature is better suited to making policy than are the voters.

Without going to the extreme of prohibiting all initiatives that affect the budget—which is unlikely to be politically feasible in any case—a very strong argument can be made for a rule requiring that future ballot initiatives that affect the budget be revenue neutral (or "self-funding"). In other words, any initiative that had the effect of lowering taxes would have to specify in detail which spending programs would be cut in order to offset the loss in revenues. And any ballot initiative that increased spending would need to specify precisely which taxes would be raised in order to pay for this spending.

To make this proposal effective, the controller's office (or some other body) would probably need to fill in some of the details regarding the budgetary consequences of a ballot initiative after the initiative received the sufficient number of signatures but before the initiative appeared on the ballot. The sponsors of an initiative might thus write that a new spending program would be funded by an increase in the sales tax rate, with the controller's office responsible for ruling on how large a sales tax increase would be required to fund the new program. The initiative would then go to the voters with the controller's numbers on what would be required to make the initiative revenue neutral.

Although requiring revenue neutral ballot initiatives would not end all of the dynamics wherein interest groups have incentives to use the initiative process instead of reaching a compromise at the legislative level, the proposal would at least counteract the consequences wherein voter psychology and the isolation effect make it overly easy to pass budget-affecting ballot initiatives. A proposal for revenue-neutral ballot initiatives should thus ameliorate at least some of the dynamics resulting in legislative gridlock and irresponsible management of California's budget crises.

Adopt Budgetary Auto-Adjusters

Another approach for reforming California's fiscal constitution would employ the use of "budgetary auto-adjusters."[15] In essence, budgetary auto-adjusters are proposals for changing the default policy outcomes that occur in the absence of legislative action. As this chapter is being written, California's legislature has again missed its constitutional deadline for passing a budget. As Democrats and Republicans bicker about how to resolve the state's massive budget shortfall, the state's financial picture continues to deteriorate, generating uncertainty about the future of both tax and spending policies.

Imagine an alternative scenario wherein appointed budgetary officials adjusted tax rates and/or spending authorizations based on formulas previously adopted by the legislature. In the absence of affirmative legislative action, this default budget would be adopted and would remain in effect until amended by the legislature.

In order to be effective, the baseline (or default) budget would be set based on prespecified formulas for how tax and spending policies should be adjusted to reflect changing economic conditions. When the state economy entered a downturn, the appointed budgetary officials would be charged with raising the tax rates and/or reducing spending authorizations in the manner specified by prior legislation so that the baseline budget would remain balanced. Hence, the authorization formulas would need to be set so as to enact some combination of: tax rates being raised during downturns and lowered during upturns, and/or spending authorizations being reduced during downturns and increased during upturns.

In addition to its effects on the formal budget process, creating an official baseline budget would have further consequences because what constitutes a "tax cut," "tax hike," "cut in spending," "or spending increase" entirely depends on what figures are used for the default levels of taxes and spending. These terms are crucial for the way in which the budget process is perceived. For instance, a majority of Republicans in the state legislature have pledged not to support any "tax hikes." But what do we mean by the term "tax hike" in an environment where the ordinary workings of the business cycle are constantly changing the relationship between tax rates and revenues raised?

The current political understanding of the budgetary baseline in California appears to be based on a notion that tax rates are to be held constant (while revenues fluctuate with the business cycle) and that spending levels are gradually increased based on prior authorizations. Yet this notion of California's budget base-

---

[15] The term "budgetary auto-adjusters" refers to a set of proposals for coping with state budget crises that the author of this chapter is developing in ongoing research.

line is essentially arbitrary. An equally plausible budgetary baseline might have tax revenues remaining constant in the absence of legislative action, with the tax rates adjusted annually in order to maintain consistency in the revenues as the economy cycles between busts and booms.

Presumably, the justification for both the two-thirds supermajority requirement for raising taxes and the Republicans' anti-tax hike pledge is to facilitate restraining the size of government. Yet cyclically adjusted tax and spending levels are a much better measure for the size of government than are current-year tax and spending levels. Under the current system, fiscal conservatives have little power to prevent spending increases during economic boom years as the legislature enjoys extra revenues as long as tax rates are kept constant. Instead, fiscal conservatives primarily fight against tax rate increases during economic downturns, as this is the only time in which the conservative minority coalition has the power to restrain the size of government.

California's existing understanding of its budgetary baseline thus has the effect of concentrating debates about the size of government into occurring primarily during bust years. Unsurprisingly, the legislature finds it very difficult to resolve these deep ideological debates under the short time requirements allowed to pass a budget following a downturn in revenues. Long periods of impasse followed by irresponsible budgets that rely on borrowing and gimmicks are the almost inevitable result.

Moving toward a system of budgetary auto-adjusters would thus have at least three advantages over California's existing budgetary process. First, the legislature would find it easier to pass budgets during bust years (or to allow the default budget to go into effect) thus reducing the use of borrowing and gimmicks. By ending the dynamics that have led the state legislature to repeatedly miss its constitutional deadline for passing budgets, a system of budgetary auto-adjusters might help restore California's credit-worthiness and the voters' trust in state government.

Second, debates about the proper size of state government would no longer be forced into a compressed process with looming deadlines. Under a system of budgetary auto-adjusters, these debates could occur at any point during the economic cycle and would be determined more by changing voter preferences rather than by changing economic conditions. In place of the current system where governors and legislators who happen to take office during boom years are able to enact their preferences for new spending programs and tax cuts, while governors and legislators in office during bust years must take the blame for enacting painful coping measures, a system of budgetary auto-adjusters would help to equalize both opportunity and blame. In this manner, budgetary auto-adjusters would enhance the accountability of elected officials to voters.

Third, adopting a system of budgetary auto-adjusters should make it easier to predict the future course of both tax and spending policy. The current budget process creates built-in uncertainty as the legislature regularly increases spending while lowering taxes during boom years, only to reverse course to enact a combination of tax hikes and spending cuts during economic downturns. Increasing the predictability of tax and spending policy would improve the economy as businessmen and investors would find it easier to plan. Similarly, increasing the predictability of spending authorizations would help program managers better utilize their funds. Under the current system, there are far too many stories like buildings being constructed during upturns and only to be left vacant during downturns as budgets are cut.

References

Ackerman, Bruce. 2006. *Before the Next Attack: Preserving Civil Liberties in an Age of Terrorism*. New Haven: Yale University Press.

Aradhna, Krishna, and Joel Slemrod. 2003. "Behavioral Public Finance: Tax Design as Price Presentation." *International Tax and Public Finance*, 189.

Baron, Jonathan, and Edward J. McCaffery. 2006. "Isolation Effects in Action: Uncovering Hidden Taxes." *Journal of Behavioral Decision Making* 19:1.

————. 2006. "Thinking About Tax." *Psychology, Public Policy, and Law* 12:106.

Boylan, Richard T. 2008. "Political Distortions in State Forecasts." *Public Choice* 136:411.

California Department of Finance. 2006. *Historical Data Budget Expenditures*. Available at http://www.dof.ca.gov/Budget/BudgetCharts/chart-b.pdf.

Congressional Budget Office. 2007. *The Long Term Budget Outlook*. Washington, D.C.

Farkas, Sarah, Karen Lyons, and Nicholas Johnson. 2007. *The Property Tax Circuit Breaker: An Introduction and Survey of Current Programs*. Center on Budget and Policy Priorities. Available at www.cbpp.org/3-21-07sfp.htm.

Garrett, Elizabeth. 2005. "Hybrid Democracy." *George Washington University Law Review* 73:1096.

Giertz, J. Fred. 2006. "The Property Tax Bound." *National Tax Journal* 59:698.

Gordon, Tracy M., Jaime Caleja Alderate, Patrick J. Murphy, Jon Sonstelle, and Pin Zhang. 2007. *Fiscal Realities: Budget Tradeoffs in California Government*. San Francisco: Public Policy Institute of California. Available at www.ppic.org/main/publications.asp?i=578.

McCubbins, Mathew D. 1995. "Putting the State Back ito State Government: The Constitution and the Budget." In *Constitutional Reform in California: Making State Government More Effective and Responsive*, ed. Bruce Cain and Rodger Noll. Berkeley, Calif.: University of California Institute of Governmental Studies.

Musso, Juliet, Elizabeth Graddy, and Jennifer Grizard. 2006. "State Budgetary Processes and Reforms: The California Story." *Public Budgeting & Finance* 26:1.

Legislative Analyst's Office. 2007. *California Spending Plan 2007-08: The Budget Act and Related Legislation*. Sacramento, Calif. Available at http://www.lao.ca.gov/2007/spend_plan/spending_plan_07-08.pdf.

National Association of State Budget Officers. 2004. *Budgeting Amid Fiscal Uncertainty: Ensuring Budget Stability by Focusing on the Long Run*. Washington, D.C. Available at http://www.nasbo.org.

————. 2008. *The Fiscal Survey of the States*. Washington, D.C. Available at http://www.nasbo.org.

Sheffrin, Steven M. 2004. "State Budget Deficit Dynamics and the California Debacle." *Journal of Economic Perspectives* 18:205.

Sjoquist, David L., and Sally Wallace. 2003. "Capital Gains: Its Recent, Varied, and Growing (?) Impact on State Revenues." *State Tax Notes* 30:497.

Sobel, Russell S., and Gary A. Wagner. 2003. "Cyclical Variability in State Government Revenue: Can Tax Reform Reduce It?" *State Tax Notes* 29:569.

Stark, Kirk J. 2001. "The Right to Vote on Taxes." *Northwestern University Law Review* 96:191.

Vasché, Jon D., and Brad Williams. 2005. "Revenue Volatility in California." *State Tax Notes* 36:35.

Zodrow, George R. 2007. "The Property Tax Incidence Debate and the Mix of State and Local Finance of Local Public Expenditures." *CESifo Economic Studies* 53:495.

Zuckerman, Stephen. 2004. *State Responses to Budget Crises in 2004: California.* Washington, D.C.: The Urban Institute. Available at http://www.urban.org/UploadedPDF/410948_CA_budget_crisis.pdf.

Section II. Economic Impacts

Chapter 5

The Evolution of Proposition 13

David R. Doerr[1]

No one looks the same as they did 30 years ago. Neither does Proposition 13. It has evolved as a result of changes made by voters, and through interpretation by the legislature, the State Board of Equalization, and the courts. Most of the provisions of the proposition have changed to some degree, but the core elements of a general 1% tax rate limit and an acquisition value assessment system for local real property remain basically the same.

This presentation will focus on the changes in the allocation of property tax revenue, the changes in the definition of change of ownership and new construction, the evolution of a fiscal tool stabilizing property tax revenue, and whether it caused any shift in tax burden over time. But first, a brief look at the property tax prior to June 6, 1978.

---

[1] Chief Consultant, Assembly Revenue and Taxation Committee, 1963-May of 1987; Chief Tax Consultant, California Taxpayers' Association, August of 1987-present.

The Property Tax before Proposition 13

In reviewing the evolution of Proposition 13, it is instructive to look at the *ad valorem* property tax system that existed prior to the passage of the initiative. It is not a pretty picture. The property tax was a major political issue from 1965 to 1978. Ronald Reagan made property tax reform one of the central issues in his campaign for governor. Some of the problems:

- **Favoritism and Corruption**. During the 1965-1978 period, two assessors from major counties were sent to prison, one major county assessor under investigation committed suicide, and another assessor from a major county resigned under investigation and was not indicted. What helped favoritism flourish was that property was assessed on a subjective basis, on an opinion of value. Proposition 13 ushered in a more objective standard, with local real property generally assessed on sales price.

- **Assessment Inequities**. During this period, the Assembly Revenue and Taxation Committee periodically obtained the result of samplings of individual local assessments in various counties by the State Board of Equalization, as part of the board's intercounty equalization responsibility. These samples showed properties being assessed at from 2% to 200% of value. Coefficients of dispersion, which is a way of measuring assessment uniformity, ranged from 7% to 37% in the three years prior to 1978. If all properties were assessed uniformly, the coefficient of dispersion would be zero. Only one county, Marin, had a coefficient of dispersion below 10%. In San Francisco, it was 21%.

- **Assessment Levels Well Below Statutory Requirements**. Prior to the passage of Proposition 13, state law required property to be assessed at 25% of value. This practice was to fool most of the voters, who were unaware of the legal requirement, to make it look like they were getting a good deal. In fact, the State Board of Equalization found actual assessed values well below the 25% level. In 1977, the average statewide assessment ratio was 23% (which would be 92% on a full value basis). Currently, the board is finding most assessors to be assessing between 98% and 100% of statutory value, under the acquisition value assessment system. San Francisco still lags, at just above 95%.

- **Property-Based School Funding Declared Unconstitutional**. In 1971, the California Supreme Court declared the property tax-based school finance system unconstitutional because some schools could raise more revenue than others with equal tax effort. *Serrano v. Priest*, 487 P. 2d 1241 (1971). In a second decision in 1976, the court ruled that a legislative fix did not solve the problem. Before a second legislative fix (AB 65 of 1977) could be tested in court (John McDermott, an attorney for the plaintiffs, said it did not comply), it was superseded by the passage of Proposition 13.

- **Property Tax Rates Higher in Urban Core Areas**. Prior to the passage of Proposition 13, property tax rates varied widely between urban areas and other regions of the state. Up to 2-1 disparities could be found. As urban core areas generally had higher tax rates, this led to another form of fiscalization of land use, by encouraging investment and housing outside the central cities.

• **Heavy Tax Burden**. Perhaps the most significant property tax problem from 1956 to 1978 was the heavy tax burden on property owners. Table 1 illustrates this burden in today's terms. If the median value home in 2006 was taxed using 1977's average tax rate and assessment ratio, the tax would be over $13,000, rather than just over $3,000. Compounding this problem was the cyclical reassessment plan used by most assessors that could cause property taxes to more than double in one year. Even worse, if a home was on land not zoned for homes, the assessor often would be valuing the property under the "highest and best use" theory of assessing then in use, as a site for a gas station or apartment house. This would result in a huge property tax bill, forcing the homeowner to sell.

In view of these problems, it is not surprising that a widespread cross-section of Californians came to believe a quote offered by University of California Economics Professor Malcolm Davisson to the Assembly Revenue and Taxation Committee, to wit: "The general property tax has only two faults: first, it is wrong in theory; and second, it doesn't work in practice."

Changes in the Allocation of Property Tax Revenue

Section 1 of Proposition 13 required the property tax to be "apportioned according to law." The legislative counsel advised lawmakers that the phrase "according to law" gave the legislature the responsibility for allocating the property tax (Opinion 17388, dated December 29, 1977). (See Revenue and Taxation Code Sections 95 through 100 for provisions allocating the property tax.)

As a practical matter, the state had to allocate the property tax. Requiring all local jurisdictions to agree on a formula was too cumbersome to be practical. Jurisdictions with little dependence on the property tax would be able to hold others hostage unless they received a large share.

If one local government agency (such as a county) had the responsibility, the allocating agency likely would take more than its fair share, considering the competition among local units for scarce property tax dollars. As it was, some counties took more than the state formula provided. State audits caught and corrected this practice. At one point, the Department of Finance found Los Angeles County giving itself $25 million a year more than it was entitled.

In designing the allocation formula, the legislature looked at alternative models. One plan would have divided the property tax equally among various levels of government (for example, counties would get 30%, cities would get 12%, schools would get 53%t, etc.). This idea was rejected by the Proposition 13 conference committee after loud protests from local jurisdictions that would have lost a substantial amount of property tax. This formula also would have resulted in some local jurisdictions getting more than they lost from the passage of Proposition 13.

Table 1. Comparison of Property Tax Bill Under Pre-Proposition 13 and Post-Proposition 13 Assessments*

	2006-07 Using Pre-Prop. 13 Method	2006-07 Using Post-Prop. 13 Method
California Median Home Value	$ 556,430	$ 556,430
Assessment Ratio	92.0 %	51.3 %
Assessed Value	$ 511,915	$ 285,448
Average Tax Rate	2.7 %	1.1 %
Annual Property Tax Bill	$ 13,668	$ 3,129
Monthly Property Tax Bill	$ 1,139	$ 261

*The assessment ratio for the "Pre-Prop. 13" column is from the 1976-77 State Board of Equalization Annual Report, Table 13 (the BOE percentage was multiplied by a factor of four to account for full-value assessment). The assessment ratio for the "Post-Prop. 13" column is calculated by dividing the assessed value of homeowner-occupied properties (as determined in the State Board of Equalization Assessed Value of Home-owner-Occupied Properties report) by the market value of homeowner-occupied property (the market value can be determined by multiplying the number of Homeowner-Occupied Properties by the California Median Home Sales Price).

During discussions of the issue, Senate President Pro Tem James Mills was very critical of legislative staff for even suggesting this alternative.

The only politically feasible allocation scheme, and the one adopted in SB 154 of 1978, was to give all local jurisdictions the same proportionate share of the property tax that existed before Proposition 13 passed. (For cities, counties, and districts, the average percentage in the prior three years was used, at the request of Senator Mills, who wanted to help jurisdictions in his San Diego County district.)

This allocation formula was justified on the basis of "need," and jurisdictions levying high property taxes prior to 1978 got a proportionately larger share than those that levied low property taxes. The formula has come under criticism for giving some counties a much larger share of the property tax than other counties.

The allocation formula has been the subject of more legislation than any other feature of Proposition 13. However, there have been few court decisions on this part of the initiative.

In 1979, the legislature, with AB 8, made two significant changes in the allocation formula. Allocation was shifted to a "*situs*" basis for growth, so fast-growing jurisdictions would get a greater share of the property tax to pay for the costs of growth. This change was accomplished by allocating the property tax proportionally based on pre-1978 shares for the property tax in each tax rate area, rather than the prior proportionate share of total countywide property tax revenue.

Provisions also were included to allocate revenues when there is a jurisdictional change (such as an annexation or creation of a new city) or a transfer of services.

The second change made by AB 8 in the allocation formula was to shift a portion of property tax revenues allocated to schools in 1978 to cities, counties, and districts for 1979 and thereafter. For cities, the amount shifted equaled 82.91% of the funds that cities received in the 1978 "bailout." For counties, the shift equaled 100% of their "bailout," adjusted for specified health and welfare costs. Special districts got 95.24% of their "bailout" in shifted property tax revenue, subject to further allocation by counties. These shifts reduced the schools' share of the property tax from 54% to 32%.

The legislature also included in AB 8 a provision known as "the deflator." The deflator was designed to work if state revenue, as estimated by the Organization Responsible for Accurate and Comprehensive Long-Range Estimates (ORACLE), fell below a specified level. In that event, local subventions would be reduced. The deflator was never activated, and it was repealed in 1984 by AB 1849 (Assembly Committee on Local Government).

Almost immediately, a group of cities that did not levy property taxes in 1977 or before began agitating for a share of the property tax. Since the property tax had been allocated based on historical shares, and these cities had no historical share, originally they did not receive any of the allocated property tax revenues.

These cities argued that the situation was unfair, because the residents of these cities were paying the same 1% tax rate as residents of other cities. However, allocation of the property tax is a "zero sum" game—for every jurisdiction that gets a larger share, others have to lose an equal amount. After several unsuccessful tries, these cities finally gained a share of the property tax. In 1984, the legislature and governor enacted SB 794 (Senate Committee on Local Government) to allocate a share of the property tax to Yorba Linda, a nonproperty-tax city in Orange County, based on a 0.1% property tax rate. In 1987, SB 709 (Lockyer) allocated a share of the property tax, also based on a 0.1% property tax rate, to all "no and low" property tax cities, phased in over 10 years. In 1988, the formula was refined by shortening the phase-in period (AB 1197, Brown).

As a result, more than 30 small- to medium-sized cities (mostly in Los Angeles County) ended up with more property tax revenue than they received prior to passage of Proposition 13.

In 1992 and 1993 the legislature shifted back to schools approximately the same percentage of property tax that had been shifted from schools to other local agencies in 1979. This shift, known as the Education Revenue Augmentation Fund, or ERAF, was done to reduce the state's budget deficit, because schools need less state support when they get added property tax revenue.

This reverse shift was highly controversial and was fought vigorously by local agencies. After agonizing over her vote, Assemblywoman Debra Bowen cast the deciding vote to approve the 1993 shift. Legislation to reshift revenue—in whole or in part—from schools back to other local agencies failed in every session from 1993 through 1998.

In 1999, the legislature gave cities and counties $150 million in one-time ERAF relief as part of the budget agreement (AB 1661, Torlakson) and asked the legislative analyst to conduct a study of property tax allocation (AB 676, Brewer).

To help balance the deficit-ridden 2004-05 and 2005-06 state budgets, the legislature again raided local coffers and shifted $1.3 million each year from local agencies to schools. Cities, counties, and special districts were hit up for $350 million each per year, and redevelopment agencies had to shift $250 million (SB 1096, Senate Budget and Fiscal Review Committee). Also, state subventions to replace revenue losses to local governments due to a car tax reduction (from 2% to 0.65% of a vehicle's value) were replaced by a shift of school property taxes from schools to cities and counties.

In exchange for all this shifting, the legislature placed SCA 4 (Torlakson) on the ballot to prevent further shifting of city and county property tax revenue. Approved by voters as Proposition 1A in November 2004, the measure prohibits the legislature from passing a bill reducing any local agency's share of the property tax, except for two years out of 10 under specified conditions. Proposition 1A won in a landslide, with 83.7% of the voters in support.

For a number of years, San Diego County worked to get a legal challenge of the property tax allocation formula to court. The county argued that it was unfair for the state to allocate more property tax to some counties than to others.

However, a case from Rancho Cucamonga reached the courts first. In 1991, the Fourth District Court of Appeal sustained the constitutionality of the allocation system in *Rancho Cucamonga v. Mackzum*, 46 Cal. Rptr. 2d 448 (4th Dist. 1991).

Evolution of the Definition of Change of Ownership

Change of ownership became the primary reappraisal trigger under Proposition 13. Determining what is and what is not a reassessable change of ownership is not an easy task due to myriad transfer techniques and the complexity of the change-of-ownership law. Initially, the Task Force on Property Tax Administration, which developed the basic implementation plan adopted by the legislature in 1979, set out to distill the basic characteristics of a change of ownership and to embody them in a single three-part test.

The task force concluded that a change of ownership is a transfer that has all three of the following characteristics:

- It transfers a present interest in real property;
- It transfers the beneficial use of the property; and
- The property rights transferred are substantially equivalent in value to the fee interest.

The legislature adopted this verbatim from the Task Force Report (see Revenue and Taxation Code Section 60).

For corporations, the legislature added a second change-of-ownership trigger (Revenue and Taxation Code Section 64). Even though shareholders have no legal rights to corporate real property, all corporate property was reassessed when a corporation or single person gained control of more than 50% of the voting stock of another corporation.

To further clarify whether transactions were or were not changes of ownership, a number of examples of each were added to statute (Revenue and Taxation Code Sections 61, 62, and 63). For example, a lease (including renewal options) for 35 years or more became a change of ownership. Transfers of property between spouses were not. Transfers into trusts were not changes of ownership if either the trust is revocable or the creator of the trust is the sole beneficiary during his or her lifetime.

The creation or renewal of a possessory interest also was a change of ownership. The original definition included sublease portions of possessory interests. Taxpayers, such as Pier 39 in San Francisco, objected, arguing that the sublease didn't meet the general test of a change of ownership.

As a result, the legislature revised the definition, providing that a sublease of a taxable possessory interest may or may not trigger a change-of-ownership reassessment, depending on the length of the sublease (SB 44, Kopp, of 1996).

Proposition 13 has been changed several times to remove types of property from a change-of-ownership reassessment. Proposition 58 of 1986 placed in the state constitution the original 1978 statutory interspousal exemption, and excluded from reassessment transfers between parents and children of dwellings and up to $1 million of other property. Voters approved Proposition 193 in 1996 to extend the parent-child transfer exclusion to grandparents and grandchildren whose parents are deceased.

In 2003, the Board of Equalization adopted a rule (462.240)—over the objections of county assessors, who asserted the board did not have authority—exempting transfers between registered domestic partners from change-of-ownership reassessments. Proponents argued that registered domestic partners should be treated the same as married couples. In 2005, the legislature codified this exemption in statute (SB 565, Migden). Again, assessors claimed that the exemption was illegal, and they went to court. In *Michael V. Strong v. State Board of Equalization*, 66 Cal. Rptr. 3d 657 (3d Dist. 2007), the Third District Court of Appeal said the legislature can ratify illegal regulations, and that Proposition 13 was a limitation to tax, and thus the legislature had the authority to create the domestic partners exclusion by statute rather than by constitutional amendment. In 2007, the legislature made this change-of-ownership exclusion retroactive to 2000 (SB 559, Kehoe).

In 2007, the parent-to-child change-of-ownership exemption was extended to foster children (AB 402, Ma).

A change-of-ownership issue unresolved as of mid-2008 was whether a transfer of a life estate in property is a transfer subject to reassessment. While the 1978-79 Task Force and the legislature said the transfer of property with a reserved life estate is not a change of ownership, they were silent on the transfers of life estates. However, they provided that a lease of less than 35 years is not a change of ownership.

The Board of Equalization and assessors have been operating as if all transfers of life estates are changes of ownership. However, in *Steinhart v. County of Los Angeles*, 155 66 Cal. Rptr. 3d 458 (2d Dist. 2007), *cert. granted*, 172 P.3d 400 (Dec. 10, 2007), the Second District Court of Appeal ruled that such transfers are not changes of ownership. In December 2007, the state Supreme Court agreed to review the decision.

It is often incorrectly presumed that changes of ownership will always produce more revenue for government due to a higher assessment. This is not true. A rule of thumb: If the market value is higher than the base-year value, the government will get more money. Conversely, if the market value is less than the Proposition 13 base-year value, government will lose money. This will occur because the transfer creates a new (and in these transfers, a lower) base-year value. Thus, the assessed value will not be allowed to increase to the original Proposition 13 base-year value.

Amendments were added in 1986 (Proposition 60) and 1988 (Proposition 90) to allow homeowners over the age of 55 to move to comparable dwellings and transfer their base-year value to the new residence within a two-year period. The right was unconditional for intracounty moves, but must be authorized by the receiving county for moves from one county to another. Severely disabled homeowners of any age also were covered by this exclusion.

In addition, change of ownership does not include the acquisition of property comparable to that taken in eminent domain proceedings (Proposition 3 of June 1982), acquisition in the same county of property comparable to that damaged by a disaster (Proposition 50 of 1986) and acquisition in a different county (if allowed by the county) of property comparable to that damaged by a disaster (Proposition 171 of 1993).

Without constitutional authorization, the legislature exempted transfers of a mobile home park to a nonprofit corporation formed by the tenants of the park and, under certain conditions, of transfers of spaces in a mobile home park to the tenants occupying those spaces (Revenue and Taxation Code Section 62.1).

The courts also have been busy attempting to define what is and is not a reassessable change of ownership. Some key decisions:

In *Sav-On Drugs, Inc. v. County of Orange*, 236 Cal. Rptr. 100 (4th Dist. 1987), an appellate court said a Section 64 change of ownership occurred when there was a corporate merger where shareholders of the acquired corporation became minority shareholders in the merged corporation.

In *E. Gottschalk and Co., Inc. v. County of Merced*, 242 Cal. Rptr. 526 (5th Dist. 1987), an appellate court stated that the provisions of Sections 61 and 62, providing that the creation of a lease of 35 years or more was a change of ownership, were a reasonable interpretation of Proposition 13. At issue was a 30-year shopping center lease with two 10-year options to renew.

In *Title Insurance and Trust Co. v. County of Riverside*, 767 P.2d 1148 (1989), the California Supreme Court, in a decision written by Justice Stanley Mosk, ruled that when a corporation acquires control of another corporation, properties owned by subsidiaries of the acquired corporation are subject to a change-of-ownership reassessment.

In *Kraft, Inc. v. County of Orange*, 268 Cal. Rptr. 643 (4th Dist. 1990), an appellate court held that reassessment of property of a corporation is triggered upon acquisition by another corporation, notwithstanding the fact that stockholders of the acquired corporation have a majority interest in the acquiring corporation. The case stemmed from the merger of Kraft and Dart Industries into a new corporation, Dart and Kraft, Inc. (DKI), with former Kraft shareholders controlling 51.5% of DKI stock. Kraft contended that no change in corporate control occurred, because Kraft shareholders became majority shareholders of DKI and continued to control Kraft indirectly. The court said: "Kraft misses the point. The same shareholders did maintain control, but a new corporation obtained direct control."

In *Howard v. County of Amador,* 269 Cal. Rptr. 807 (3d Dist. 1990), an appellate court rejected Amador County's contention that the transfer of long-term fixed mineral interests in a property requires a reassessment of all interests in a property. However, the court found that the transfer of fixed-term mineral rights is a change of ownership for the specific mineral right transferred.

In *Shuwa Investments Corp. v. County of Los Angeles*, 2 Cal. Rptr. 2d 783 (2d Dist. 1991), an appellate court found that a complicated step transaction by which Shuwa Investments Corporation gained full control of the ARCO Plaza complex in Los Angeles triggered a full change of ownership.

Prior to the transaction, ARCO and Bank of America each owned 50% of a partnership that owned ARCO Plaza. Shuwa Investments gained control of the property in a three-step transaction in which: (1) ARCO sold its partnership interests to Shuwa; (2) Shuwa and Bank of America liquidated the partnership and received 50%t undivided interests in the property; and (3) Bank of America sold its 50% interest to Shuwa.

In *Pacific Southwest Realty Co. v. County of Los Angeles*, 820 P.2d 1046 (1991), the California Supreme Court reversed a lower court decision and held that sales and leaseback transactions are changes in ownership. At issue was the reassessment of the Security Pacific Bank building in downtown Los Angeles after its sale and leaseback in 1984. The $310 million sale of the building included a reservation of an estate of 73% of the property for a specified number of years.

In discussing Section 60's "transfer of a present interest in real property" test, Justice Stanley Mosk wrote: "Plaintiff's contention that it did not convey a present interest in real property is simply incorrect and cannot forestall a conclusion that a transfer of a present interest in real property occurred. Plaintiff did not retain the same interest when it sold its fee and reserved an estate for years. The entire fee was transferred to Metropolitan Life. The simultaneous creation of a different interest in plaintiff will not defeat the first prong of Section 60."

In 1997 and 1998, the State Board of Equalization revised its change-of-ownership rules to make them clearer and easier to understand. For example, Rule 462.180, which clarifies various aspects of legal entity transfers, was amended to include limited liability companies.

Evolution of the Definition of New Construction

Since Proposition 13 did not define "new construction," the matter of what type of "new construction" should trigger a new assessment remains an issue at this writing. There was no question that any addition to land would give rise to a new assessment. But what about remodeling?

Initially, the State Board of Equalization, by Rule 463, took the position that any alteration of an existing improvement that extended the economic life of the property triggered a reassessment.

In 1979, the legislature specifically rejected the BOE approach, and provided that only a major rehabilitation of an improvement would create a "reassessable event." A major rehabilitation was defined as a renovation that converted an improvement to the equivalent of a new improvement (see Revenue and Taxation Code Section 70).

For multi-year new construction, the construction in progress on the lien date is appraised at its full value, and on the date of completion, the entire property is reappraised.

Voters adopted several amendments to Proposition 13 that provided for or authorized exclusions from a "new construction" reassessment. These exclusions included specified reconstruction after a disaster (Proposition 8 of November 1978), specific seismic reinforcements (Proposition 23 of 1984), fire extinguishing systems (Proposition 31 of 1984), and construction for making a dwelling more accessible to disabled people (Proposition 110 of 1990, and Proposition 177 of 1994).

In 1998, voters approved Proposition 1, authorizing the legislature to exempt from new construction the replacement or repair of a structure on substantially environmentally damaged property, after remediation of the problem.

An unusual incident involving the interpretation of what constitutes new construction occurred in the early 1980s, when Los Angeles County Assessor Alex Pope sued the State Board of Equalization over advice given by BOE Assessment Standards Chief Verne Walton in 1980 in Assessors' Letter 80-77.

Since advice by the board to assessors through letters and assessment manuals does not have the same force of law as a board rule, it was surprising for an assessor to sue over an assessors' letter.

At issue was the treatment of construction in progress. Revenue and Taxation Code Section 71 provided that construction in progress be appraised each year, and that upon the date of completion, the entire portion of newly constructed property would be reappraised. In Assessors' Letter 80-77, the BOE stated that when a large project is completed in distinct stages, with some portions available for occupancy prior to completion of the total project, it is proper to assign a base year to the completed portions. Pope disagreed, saying there should be a final reappraisal of all phases when the total project is completed.

The Second District Court of Appeal in 1983 sided with the board, saying the board's interpretation of its rule was consistent with legislative intent. *Pope v. State Board of Equalization,* 194 Cal. Rptr. 883 (2d Dist. 1983).

Proposition 13 Adds Stability to Property Tax

One of the features of Proposition 13 that was not apparent when it passed was the long-term stabilization of property tax revenues. No one mentioned this as an advantage in the campaign, nor was it mentioned in any analysis of the measure. Under an *ad valorem* system, revenues are much more volatile, growing fast when real estate values boom, and falling in real estate downturns, such as the one we're in now.

Proposition 13's acquisition value assessment system acts in a counter-cyclical manner to provide stability in the flow of property tax revenue to local government. Acquisition value assessments have worked in the nature of a reservoir by keeping an untapped reserve of value that will accrue to local entities upon changes in ownership.

In years of high inflation of real estate values, Proposition 13 acts as a brake, holding back money that otherwise would have been generated by rapidly growing assessments under an *ad valorem* tax. Conversely, in times of falling property values, assessment growth continues under an acquisition value system, since the new, substantially higher values from changes of ownership, new construction, and the 2% inflation factor are likely to exceed the Proposition 8 decline-in-value assessments.

For example, assume that there is a 10% drop in market values, and a property worth $300,000 falls to $270,000 in value from one year to the next. Assume that the property's base-year value is $100,000. When it changes ownership, the value on the roll goes up $170,000 under the acquisition value system, rather than falling $30,000, as it would under the *ad valorem* system.

Table 2 illustrates the "reservoir effect" of Proposition 13. During economic downturns, when real estate market values declined—at times as much as 4.5% (1993-94)—because of Proposition 13, the average assessed value of an individual homeowner-occupied property grew for that same time period (3.9% in 1993-94, see Table 2).

A Shift in Tax Burden?

Has the evolution of Proposition 13 caused a shift in the tax burden among classes of properties? When Proposition 13 passed, there was concern that the initiative would result in a shift of the property tax burden to homeowners. The Property Tax Administration Task Force, formed to implement the assessment

Table 2. Comparison of Proposition 13 Homeowner-Occupied Property and California Median Home Sales Price

Year	Assessed Value of a Single Homeowner-Occupied Property[a]	Percent Increase by Year	California Median Sales Price[b]	Percent Increase by Year
1979-80[c]	$ 11,357	-	$ 84,150	-
1980-81[c]	$ 13,076	15.1	$ 99,550	18.3
1981-82	$ 57,120	9.2	$ 107,710	8.2
1982-83	$ 61,610	7.9	$ 111,800	3.8
1983-84	$ 64,282	4.3	$ 114,370	2.3
1984-85	$ 69,258	7.7	$ 114,260	(0.1)
1985-86	$ 74,326	7.3	$ 119,860	4.9
1986-87	$ 79,712	7.2	$ 133,640	11.5
1987-88	$ 86,551	8.6	$ 142,060	6.3
1988-89	$ 93,318	7.8	$ 168,200	18.4
1989-90	$ 103,768	11.2	$ 196,120	16.6
1990-91	$ 113,488	9.4	$ 193,770	(1.2)
1991-92	$ 121,777	7.3	$ 200,660	3.6
1992-93	$ 130,412	7.1	$ 197,030	(1.8)
1993-94	$ 135,503	3.9	$ 188,240	(4.5)
1994-95	$ 139,164	2.7	$ 185,010	(1.7)
1995-96	$ 142,154	2.1	$ 178,160	(3.7)
1996-97	$ 145,133	2.1	$ 177,270	(0.5)
1997-98	$ 147,888	1.9	$ 186,490	5.2
1998-99	$ 155,314	5.0	$ 200,100	7.3
1999-00	$ 165,278	6.4	$ 217,510	8.7
2000-01	$ 176,946	7.1	$ 241,350	11.0
2001-02	$ 190,478	7.6	$ 262,350	8.7
2002-03	$ 203,404	6.8	$ 316,130	20.5
2003-04	$ 221,313	8.8	$ 371,520	17.5
2004-05	$ 235,854	6.6	$ 450,770	21.3
2005-06	$ 260,525	10.5	$ 522,670	16.0
2006-07	$ 285,024	9.4	$ 556,430	6.5
Average	-	7.1	-	7.5

[a]Data calculated by dividing the total value of homeowner-occupied property (see Appendix 1) by the total number of homeowner exemptions as reported in the BOE Annual Reports, Table 9.

[b]Source: Data from the California Association of Realtors.

[c]Until 1981-1982, property was assessed at 25% of "full" value. Above "Percent Increase by Year" accounts for assessment changes.

provisions of the initiative, was one of the groups worried that there might be such a shift.

For a number of years, critics of Proposition 13 have alleged that such a shift occurred. They now cite the latest figures from the State Board of Equalization that owner-occupied homes represented 34.3% of total property tax assessed values in 1979-80 and 39.3% in 2006-07.

Those figures are misleading. According to a more in-depth analysis of BOE data, published by Cal-Tax in 2008, Proposition 13 did not cause this shift, and in fact has prevented a more substantial shift to homeowners.

Further refinement of the data shows that values of owner-occupied homes grew an average of 8.3 percent a year since 1979, while values of other property subject to Proposition 13's acquisition value assessment system grew an average of 8.5% a year (Table 3).

Why are both homeowner and nonhomeowner properties subject to Proposition 13 assessment a larger percentage of the assessment roll by 2006-07? Ironically, the properties that still are assessed on an *ad valorem* basis at 100% of their value are very slow-growing. Locally assessed personal property values have grown only 4.2% a year on average, and the value of state-assessed property other than railroad property has grown only 3.4% a year. State-assessed railroad property's average growth rate has been 0.7%.

The share of the total of nonhomeowner locally assessed property subject to Proposition 13's acquisition assessment system grew from 47.4% in 1979-80 to 55.0% in 2006-07 (Figures 1 and 2). To put it another way, of property subject to Proposition 13's acquisition value assessment, the owner-occupied home share actually declined from 41.99% in 1979-80 to 41.64% in 2006-07 (Figures 3 and 4).

If Proposition 13 had not passed, the share of property tax paid both for homeowner-occupied and nonhomeowner properties (currently subject to Proposition 13) would have been greater than it is today.

Another way of looking at the comparative tax burden is to determine the percentage of market values at which properties are being assessed. Since the late 1980s, the BOE has been determining the ratio of acquisition value to market value for commercial and industrial property. This is required by federal law (the 4-R Act) to adjust the value of state-assessed railroad property. Table 4 shows this ratio for each year. Commercial and industrial property assessment averaged 75.1% of market value from 1988-89 to 2006-07.

For owner-occupied property, the average for the same period is 66.3% (Table 5). Thus, if all properties were assessed on an *ad valorem* basis (the assessment system prior to Proposition 13), homeowners would be paying a much larger percentage of the total property tax burden.

Table 3. Comparison of Growth in Assessed Value of Homeowner-Occupied Property and Nonhomeowner-Occupied Property Subject to Proposition 13 Assessment Provisions

Year	Homeowner Occupied Property*	Percent Increase by Year	All Locally Assessed Nonhomeowner Property Subject to Prop. 13**	Percent Increase by Year
1979-80	$ 45.6	-	$ 63.0	-
1980-81	$ 53.7	17.8	$ 74.7	18.6
1981-82	$ 238.1	10.8	$ 345.7	15.7
1982-83	$ 259.6	9.0	$ 392.7	13.6
1983-84	$ 273.6	5.4	$ 429.9	9.5
1984-85	$ 295.2	7.9	$ 479.0	11.4
1985-86	$ 321.1	8.8	$ 529.9	10.6
1986-87	$ 349.9	9.0	$ 578.2	9.1
1987-88	$ 386.5	10.5	$ 641.8	11.0
1988-89	$ 424.3	9.8	$ 705.2	9.9
1989-90	$ 477.1	12.4	$ 780.3	10.6
1990-91	$ 528.1	10.7	$ 878.8	12.6
1991-92	$ 573.7	8.6	$ 955.1	8.7
1992-93	$ 625.3	9.0	$ 990.1	3.7
1993-94	$ 664.7	6.3	$ 1,000.8	1.1
1994-95	$ 699.8	5.3	$ 991.7	-0.9
1995-96	$ 722.9	3.3	$ 978.1	-1.4
1996-97	$ 739.8	2.3	$ 980.5	0.2
1997-98	$ 759.8	2.7	$ 1,004.2	2.4
1998-99	$ 800.4	5.3	$ 1,046.7	4.2
1999-00	$ 856.9	7.1	$ 1,127.3	7.7
2000-01	$ 921.4	7.5	$ 1,250.7	10.9
2001-02	$ 1,001.7	8.7	$ 1,351.7	8.1
2002-03	$ 1,080.2	7.8	$ 1,516.5	12.2
2003-04	$ 1,193.1	10.5	$ 1,543.0	1.7
2004-05	$ 1,281.7	7.4	$ 1,698.1	10.1
2005-06	$ 1,422.3	11.0	$ 1,903.7	12.1
2006-07	$ 1,559.4	9.6	$ 2,185.2	14.8
Average	-	8.3	-	8.5

Note: Dollar amounts in billions.

*Source: From the State Board of Equalization Assessed Value of Properties Receiving the Homeowners' Exemption as a Percentage of Total Assessed Value.

**Sources: See Appendix 1 for a complete explanation of this table.

Figure 1. Percentage of Overall Property Taxes Borne by Homeowners and Nonhomeowners during the 1979–1980 Assessment Period

12.7%   5.6%

34.3%   47.4%

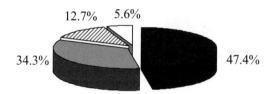

- All Locally Assessed Nonhomeowner Property
- Homeowner Occupied Property
- Locally Assessed Tangible Personal Property–Non-Prop. 13
- State Assessed Property–Non-Prop. 13, Including Railroad Values

Note: Percentages are for the 1979–1980 assessment period.
Source: State Board of Equalization; Dave Doerr, California's Tax Machine, 559–62: 2008.

Figure 2. Percentage of Overall Property Taxes Borne by Homeowners and Nonhomeowners during the 2006–2007 Assessment Period

4.0%   1.7%

39.3%   55.0%

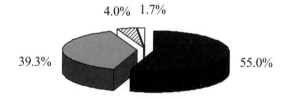

- All Locally Assessed Nonhomeowner Property Subject to Prop. 13
- Homeowner Occupied Property
- Locally Assessed Tangible Personal Property–Non-Prop. 13
- State Assessed Property–Non-Prop. 13, Including Railroad Values

Note: Percentages are for the 2006–2007 assessment period.
Source: State Board of Equalization; Dave Doerr, California's Tax Machine, 559–62: 2008.

Figure 3. Share of Property Tax Values for Properties Subject to Proposition 13 Acquisition Value Assessments, 1979–1980

42.0%   58.0%

- All Locally Assessed Nonhomeowner Property Subject to Prop. 13
- Homeowner Occupied Property

Note: Percentages are for the 1979–1980 assessment period.
Source: State Board of Equalization; Dave Doerr, California's Tax Machine. 559–62: 2008.

Figure 4. Share of Property Tax Values for Properties Subject to Proposition 13 Acquisition Value Assessments, 2006–2007

41.6%   58.4%

- All Locally Assessed Nonhomeowner Property Subject to Prop. 13
- Homeowner Occupied Property

Note: Percentages are for the 2006–2007 assessment period.
Source: State Board of Equalization; Dave Doerr, California's Tax Machine, 559–62: 2008.

Table 4. Commercial and Industrial Property Assessments as a Percentage of Market Value

Year	Assessment Ratio
1988-89	70.4
1989-90	71.1
1990-91	74.2
1991-92	74.9
1992-93	81.9
1993-94	84.9
1994-95	87.6
1995-96	86.7
1996-97	86.1
1997-98	80.6
1998-99	76.2
1999-00	75.6
2000-01	71.7
2001-02	74.9
2002-03	72.7
2003-04	71.5
2004-05	65.6
2005-06	61.0
2006-07	59.9

Notes: See Appendix 2. All Business Property Assessed values are based on BOE Roll Year assessments. Data from the State Board of Equalization Ratio of Assessed Value of Commerical/Industrial Property to Market Value as adopted by the BOE each May, which is known as the "4-R Act." (Federal law requires railroad property to be assessed at the same ratio of market value as all other business property.) Legislation requiring the BOE to determine the ratio of assessed value to market value for business property was not adopted by the legislature until 1986 in AB 2890 (Hannigan). Records for the roll years of 1986-1987 and 1987-1988 were not available at time of printing (due to a mold problem at the BOE headquarters, records were temporarily moved to storage in 2007 and were not accessible).

Table 5. Homeowner-Occupied Property Assessments as a Percentage of Market Value

Year	Homeowner Assessed Value in Proportion to Market Value
1979-80	54.0
1980-81	52.5
1981-82	53.0
1982-83	55.1
1983-84	56.2
1984-85	60.6
1985-86	62.0
1986-87	59.6
1987-88	60.9
1988-89	55.5
1989-90	52.9
1990-91	58.6
1991-92	60.7
1992-93	66.2
1993-94	72.0
1994-95	75.2
1995-96	79.8
1996-97	81.9
1997-98	79.3
1998-99	77.6
1999-00	76.0
2000-01	73.3
2001-02	72.6
2002-03	64.3
2003-04	59.6
2004-05	52.3
2005-06	49.8
2006-07	51.2
Average from 1988	66.3
Average from 1979	63.3

Chapter 6

Serrano and Proposition 13: The Importance of Asking the Right Questions

William A. Fischel[1]

The *Serrano*-Proposition 13 Hypothesis

Gary Fields, a Cornell economist and hiking buddy, used to tell me, "if you don't ask the right questions, you won't get the right answers." I submit that the right question about Proposition 13 is not what caused individual Californians to vote for it by a margin of almost two to one in 1978. As the exhaustive efforts of Jack Citrin (1985, with David Sears) have shown, there are no convincing answers to that question. The right question to ask is why almost the same group of voters a mere six years earlier had *rejected* a similar property-tax limitation by almost two to one. This question requires that we look at what was *different* in California in 1978 as opposed to 1972 (or 1968, when another property-tax limitation had also been rejected by a two to one margin).[2]

---

[1] Economics Department, Dartmouth College, Hanover, NH 03755, Bill.Fischel@ Dartmouth.edu.

[2] This note was prepared for the conference "Proposition 13 at 30: The Political, Economic and Fiscal Impacts," which was held in Berkeley, California, on June 6, 2008. I offer a brief overview of my scholarship connecting Proposition 13 with the decision in

My answer is that the implementation of the *Serrano* decision by the 1977 state legislature was the most important difference between 1972 and 1978. *Serrano* found that California's existing reliance on local property taxes to fund schools was unconstitutional. In 1972, voters in most of the school districts in California could still see a connection between what they paid in property taxes and the quality of their local public schools. Philip Watson's 1968 and 1972 property-tax limitations held few charms for the majority of voters because the initiatives would have disrupted that connection. Watson's 1% limitation on taxes (which had been endorsed by Howard Jarvis) would have limited the ability of local districts to spend what they pleased on education. Even voters without children could gain because the value of their single largest asset—their homes—would rise (or at least not fall) with better local schools.

The *Serrano* decision broke the connection between local property taxes and local school spending. This is not a tale of "unintended consequences." The litigants and judges who crafted *Serrano* deliberately sought to disconnect local taxes rates from school spending. The legislature dutifully responded with a bill in 1977 that "substantially complied" with this mandate. In order not to reduce the overall level of school spending, however, the legislature needed to continue property taxation. Local school taxes were, in effect, requisitioned by the legislature to finance education throughout the state. When home-value inflation pushed those local taxes beyond the voters' endurance, the legislature was unable to cut school taxes. Doing so would have been out of compliance with the mandates of the California Supreme Court in *Serrano*.

Proposition 13 Was Not a General Tax Revolt

Here is evidence that it was local school taxes, not other property taxes, that voters suddenly found so objectionable. After the legislature had passed AB 65, which was its attempt to comply with *Serrano*, it had to do something about the tax revolt that was brewing in 1977. Legislators knew that their constituents were unhappy with rising taxes. The surprising ease with which the Jarvis-Gann initiative qualified for the ballot indicated that an alternative had to be offered. The alternative was known as the Behr bill, after its sponsor, Marin County Senator Philip Behr. The Behr bill was a massive reduction in property taxes, almost as great as that offered by Proposition 13. Its implementation required that voters approve Proposition 8, placed on the same ballot as Proposition 13.

Serrano v. Priest, 96 Cal. Rptr. 601 (1971) ("*Serrano I*"), 135 Cal. Rptr. 345 (1976) ("*Serrano II*") (1976). For sources to back up statements in this note, see my most recent comprehensive article on the subject (Fischel 2004). Table 1 (next page) offers a chronology of events that led up to Proposition 13.

Table 1. Property-Tax Initiative and School Finance Chronology

Nov. 5, 1968	"Watson I" initiative (Proposition 9) to limit property taxes defeated: 32.0% yes; 68.0% no
August 30, 1971	*Serrano I* decided (6-1) and remanded to Los Angeles Superior Court
Nov. 7, 1972	"Watson II" initiative (Proposition 14) to limit property taxes defeated: 34.1% yes; 65.9% no
March 21, 1973	*San Antonio v. Rodriguez* decided by U.S. Supreme Court (5-4), denying *Serrano*-style equal protection claims at the federal level
April 10, 1974	Judge Bernard Jefferson rules for *Serrano* plaintiffs in Los Angeles Superior Court; defendants appeal
Dec. 30, 1976	*Serrano II* decided in favor of plaintiffs (4-3), sustaining Judge Jefferson's remedy
Sept. 2, 1977	AB 65, school finance bill intended to comply with *Serrano II,* passes legislature; property tax relief bill fails on same day
Dec. 29, 1977	"Jarvis" initiative (Proposition 13) certified for the June 1978 ballot
March 3, 1978	Governor signs "Behr Bill" (SB 1), alternative to Proposition 13, tying its implementation to passage of Proposition 8, constitutional amendment allowing "split roll," in which residential property could be taxed at a lower rate than other classifications
June 6, 1978	Proposition 13 passes: 64.8% yes; 35.2% no; Proposition 8 (and thus the Behr Bill) defeated: 47.0% yes; 53.0% no

Proposition 8 would have amended the California Constitution to permit the legislature to assess owner-occupied homes at a lower proportion of value than other components of the property-tax base. Home values had been driven up disproportionately by the general inflation that began in the early 1970s, and Proposition 8 would have amended the state constitution to permit the legislature to authorize taxation of commercial and industrial property at a higher effective rate than homes. The Behr bill also offered tax relief for renters, something that Proposition 13 ignored entirely.

The legislature designed Proposition 8 so that it deferred to Proposition 13. Proposition 8 (and hence the Behr Bill) would not become law unless it was approved by a majority of the voters *and* that majority was greater than that of Proposition 13. Because of this condition, voters who sought a property tax reduction had nothing to lose by voting for both Proposition 13 and Proposition 8. A voter interested in maximizing his or her chance of getting property tax relief would vote for both initiatives.

Proposition 8 received 47% of the votes, compared to 65% for Proposition 13. That in itself is a puzzle for people who regard Proposition 13 as a general tax revolt rather than, as I do, a selective revolt against the *Serrano* reforms. If Proposition 13 was a general tax revolt, Proposition 8 should have passed, too. Perhaps not with as large a majority as Proposition 13, given its lesser tax reduction, but it should have done better.

More striking are the data showing votes on Proposition 13 ("Jarvis") and Proposition 8 ("Behr") arrayed by school districts shown in Figure 1. The 135 districts are those identified by Stark and Zasloff (2003) as having names that were the same as a city. (Votes in 1978 were tabulated by city, not school district, so not all school districts in California could be counted.) If Proposition 13 was a general tax revolt, the cities in which Proposition 13 got the most votes should also be the cities in which Proposition 8 got the most votes. That is, the general array of points in Figure 1 should suggest a positive slope. As can be seen, however, the city-districts that most favored Proposition 13 were most opposed to Proposition 8. The negative relationship is obvious. Indeed, the inverse relationship is so strong that I initially thought I had made a sign error. Social scientists very seldom see relationships this strong.

My explanation for the negative relationship between the Proposition 8 vote and the Proposition 13 vote hinges on a particular feature of Proposition 8. Proposition 8 applied to all property taxes *except* those for education. This exclusion was necessary to preserve the legislature's response to the *Serrano* decision. AB 65 required that property taxation for schools continue, even though local discretion over school-tax rates was largely eliminated. Without property taxes, AB 65 could not be implemented, and in fact once Proposition 13 passed, AB 65 became a nullity.

My hypothesis, then, is that school districts that most favored Proposition 13 were those that were most adversely affect by AB 65, whom I refer to as "*Serrano* losers." Such districts had a large property-value per pupil. Proposition

Figure 1. Behr (Prop. 8) versus Jarvis (Prop. 13), by School District

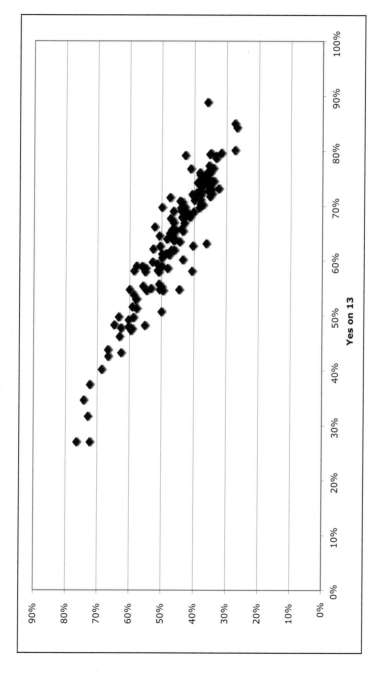

Yes on 13

Scatter diagram of citywide votes for Behr ("yes on 8") and Jarvis ("yes on 13") for Stark and Zasloff's (2004) 135-city sample.

8 gave such districts almost no tax relief at all. Hence the districts that most favored Proposition 13 (in the upper left side of Figure 1) also most opposed the other form of tax relief, Proposition 8.

I readily concede that there could be other reasons why the points in Figure 1 do not suggest a positive relationship between Proposition 13 and Proposition 8. Howard Jarvis and other proponents of Proposition 13 regarded Proposition 8 as the enemy and told supporters to oppose it. The legislature had promoted Proposition 8 as a substitute for Proposition 13, not as a complement to it. If these factors played a role in the voting, then there would be an imperfectly positive relationship between Proposition 13 and Proposition 8 voting, assuming (as I do not) that voters simply wanted a tax reduction, regardless of the source. They might have been so strong as to create a random relationship between the two. But there is nothing random-looking about the array of points in Figure 1. Proposition 13 gave relief to districts that were *Serrano* losers, while Proposition 8 did not. The nearly perfect negative relationship between Proposition 8 and Proposition 13 votes by school district is consistent with my *Serrano* story and inconsistent with the idea that California voters in 1978 just wanted a tax break.

The supposed irrationality of voters that informs much of the academic commentary on Proposition 13 has been challenged by scholarship that suggests that voting is in fact an accurate way to aggregate information and preferences. This is the implication of the median-voter theory and political prediction markets. I cannot in this space elucidate these models—an accessible source is Cass Sunstein's *Infotopia* (2006)—but I do wish to point out a feature that makes these models' application to the Proposition 13 vote more plausible.

In order for majority voting to converge on the correct outcome, voters must have access to information that is more likely true than false. Commentators on Proposition 13 have often focused on the extravagant claims of Howard Jarvis and others as a source of biased information. However, a large majority of voters had access to accurate information about the source of their tax troubles: their tax bills. Property tax bills do not simply present taxpayers with a final sum to be paid. Taxes are broken out by taxing jurisdiction. Thus taxpaying voters in Arcadia (for example) could see whether it was the levies for the city of Arcadia, the Arcadia Unified School District, the county of Los Angeles, or a special-service district that accounted for the bulk of their tax increases. They did not have to deliberate about it or read the newspaper or watch TV to find out which of their taxes was going through the roof. All they had to do was compare last year's tax bill to the current year's tax bill. It was not at all implausible that voters in school districts that were *Serrano*-losers knew that Proposition 8 would not give them much tax relief.

Voters in High-Value Districts
Turned Against the Property Tax

Other evidence that supports the *Serrano*-Proposition 13 connection is summarized in Figure 2. (This is illustrative of multiple regression analysis undertaken in Fischel 2004 and 2008.) The vertical axis is the variable "swing," which is the percentage increase in the vote for Proposition 13 in 1978 with respect to the vote for the Watson initiative in 1972. Swing is calculated for cities in Los Angeles County that correspond to school districts. (Los Angeles County had a sufficiently large number of cities and school districts to do statistical tests within the county, which was important because the Watson initiative had features that varied by county.) The horizontal axis is the taxable value per pupil for the city's school district in 1977-78. The *Serrano* court regarded value per pupil as the source of unconstitutional spending variation, and leveling the supposed advantages that this conferred on a school district was the objective of the legislature's response to *Serrano*.

Consider, for example, the upper-right point in Figure 2, the city of El Segundo. It is located just south of Los Angeles International Airport. Its school district had a large amount of taxable property (due mainly to an oil refinery) and a relatively low student enrollment (due to an aging population), giving it the highest tax base per pupil of any district in Los Angeles County. Only 22.7% of the city's voters favored the 1972 Watson initiative (compared to 34.1% of voters statewide). In 1978, however, El Segundo voted disproportionately in favor of Proposition 13, with 79.6% of voters favoring it (compared to the statewide 64.8%). El Segundo's 1972 to 1978 "swing" was the largest in Los Angeles County, 250%. (That is, 79.6 minus 22.7, divided by 22.7, equals 250%.)

Figure 2 suggests a strong, positive relationship between the 1972-to-1978 vote swing and value per pupil. This is consistent with the *Serrano*-Proposition 13 connection. Taxpayers in "property-poor" (low value per pupil) districts, such as Baldwin Park (on the lower left of Figure 2) were not as adversely affected by the *Serrano* ruling, and so their "swing" was among the lowest in Los Angeles County. (I attribute the negative swing of mostly African-American Compton, the only city in the county to have voted against Proposition 13, to Howard Jarvis's racial insensitivity.) I should note, by the way, that Baldwin Park's low "swing" does not mean that its voters opposed Proposition 13. It actually favored Proposition 13 by a 70% majority. Its low "swing" was accounted for by its relatively strong support (44%) for the 1972 Watson initiative. This is an example of why it is critical to examine the vote for Proposition 13 in the context of previous initiatives. Something *changed* between 1972 and 1978 to induce voters to change their view of local property taxes. Just asking voters why they favored or opposed Proposition 13 will overlook this crucial question.

Figure 2. Swing and Value/Pupil for 46-City Los Angeles County Sample

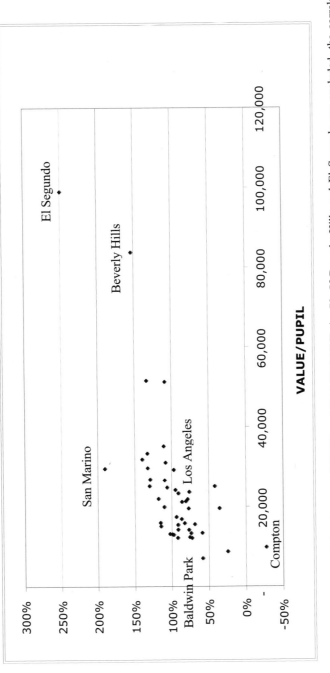

The simple correlation between SWING and VALUE/PUPIL is .72. If Beverly Hills and El Segundo are excluded, the correlation is .55.
Source: Fischel (2008).

Why the Elderly Turned against Local School Taxes

When I wrote my first article about the *Serrano*-Proposition 13 connection in 1989, the theory was regarded as a considerable novelty, to put it charitably. I had thought of it soon after Proposition 13 had passed (as had a handful of other economists), but I did not pursue it. I was sure some more obvious, less subtle explanation would come forward. But none did, and I accumulated evidence besides what I summarize here that supports it (Fischel 1989; 1996). Over time, my explanation seems to have become the conventional wisdom within public economics. That is not necessarily an enviable position. The conventional wisdom is always something to be challenged. Two thorough and resourceful challenges are articles by Kirk Stark and Jonathan Zasloff (2003) and by Isaac Martin (2006). Each raises a number of different issues, but their common element is skepticism of my exclusive focus on value per pupil as a marker for the impact of the *Serrano* decision on voter decisions.

Stark and Zasloff found that the percentage of elderly residents in the population had a larger and more statistically significant effect in explaining the vote swing from 1972 to 1978. In their regressions (and in my replication of them), using the variable "seniors" (percentage of city residents over age 65) as an independent variable to explain the vote swing eliminates the significance of value per pupil. They conclude from this that my indicator for *Serrano*-losers, districts with high value per pupil, is a red herring. In their view, some combination elderly voters, the rich, and Republicans accounted for most of the shift.

My original response to Stark and Zasloff was to point out that "seniors" and "value per pupil" were actually closely correlated. It turns out that much of the variation of value per pupil among school districts was not accounted for by the personal wealth of the residents, but by how many of their kids attended public school. Districts with many elderly people simply had fewer kids in school, and so the "per pupil" number was small and hence "value per pupil" was large. Stark and Zasloff's result was, I submitted, a simple case of multicollinearity.

Multicollinearity, however, is not the only issue. Suppose "seniors" really is the critical variable. That still requires us to address what I think is the crucial question: What was it that changed so radically between 1972 and 1978 that induced California voters to switch from property-tax defenders to property-tax rebels? The fraction of the population that was over age 65 had not changed much in six years. Inflation in home values was new, but that was a condition everywhere and anyway, the legislature knew how to deal with that. Proposition 8 would have allowed it to reduce homeowner assessments—except for school taxes.

So Stark and Zasloff's insightful critique of my work directs me back to the question of why older voters first opposed (in 1972) and then favored (in 1978) a property-tax limitation. The answer is that the major asset of most older voters is their home. Home values are much influenced by the quality of local schools, and study after study shows that older voters are supportive of local education spending when it will enhance the value of their homes. This is a subtle distinction, however. Increasing school spending across the state, which was the (ultimately failed) objective of the *Serrano* litigants, would not have excited much interest on the part of elderly voters. The value of one's home is enhanced by having schools that are relatively better than those in nearby districts. If all schools improve at the same rate, there is no special reason for homebuyers to favor one district over another, and thus no special reason for elderly voters to support local education spending.

I thus conclude that the variable "seniors" actually captures the effect of the *Serrano* decision better than value per pupil alone. The correlation with seniors and value per pupil is supplemented by the behavioral effect: Seniors were once strongly inclined to oppose tax limitations that would have undermined their local schools. *Serrano* disconnected local taxes from school spending, and homeowners without children in school became indifferent to local school quality and more sensitive to tax increases.

Isaac Martin's critique of my work also focuses on the issue of seniors versus value per pupil, but his concern is that the aggregated data that I (and Stark and Zasloff) use cannot distinguish among their effects. Martin attempts to overcome this by painstakingly recovering individual data on respondents to surveys of voters in the Proposition 13 era. My main problem with his attempt is that I don't think it makes much difference whether voters responded positively to Proposition 13 because of value per pupil or because they were elderly. Either response begs the question of why six years earlier voters with those characteristics were not eager to limit the property tax. Something changed between 1972 and 1978 to alienate both the "property rich" and the elderly communities from school property taxes. The only logical candidate was the *Serrano* decision and the inflation-driven property values that the legislature requisitioned to fund its response to it.

Martin's quest for individual voters from statewide polls is also complicated by what I see as the main reason that so many observers have missed the *Serrano*-Prop. 13 connection. The Field Poll and other statewide polls have repeatedly and extensively asked voters about their support for Proposition 13. The sample of voters for all such polls has been weighted towards the largest population centers. This makes perfectly good statistical sense. If one wants to predict a statewide election in which each vote counts the same, regardless of location within the state, a properly random sample will have most respondents from the Los Angeles and San Francisco areas.

The problem with this procedure is that it does not facilitate a test of the *Serrano*-Proposition 13 connection. The California Supreme Court directed its *Serrano* remedy towards school districts, not toward individuals. The issue was fiscal and spending differences between school districts, not inequalities within individual school districts. The fact that residents within the Los Angeles Unified School District, for example, might have different opinions about their school taxes or school spending was of no importance to the *Serrano* court. Thus the only way to test whether *Serrano* had anything to do with the success of

Proposition 13 is to examine votes by school districts. But the Field Poll and others draw most of their observations from only a handful of large school districts, making it nearly impossible to get a representative sample of voters for most of the districts in the state. This is reflected in Isaac Martin's data. Fully half of his 369 voters that he was able to extract from the Field Poll lived in only two school districts, Los Angeles and San Francisco. Of the 39 districts represented in his sample, more than half are represented by fewer than four voters. This is not a useful way to infer districtwide votes.

Conclusion: The Importance of Asking the Right Question

Statewide polls have not asked the right questions about Proposition 13. This is not merely an academic issue. By persistently asking the wrong questions, polls have misled scholars and public officials about the causes of Proposition 13. California voters are thought to be irrational or excessively selfish or systematically misled by demagogues like Howard Jarvis. As such, officials despair of fixing the adverse effects of Proposition 13. But if the *Serrano* story has more than a grain of truth, voters might be willing to modify Proposition 13. A modification of the *Serrano* decision to allow local property taxes to connect more closely to local school spending could convince voters to accept modifications of Proposition 13. But we will not know that until there is more widespread understanding of the true causes of Proposition 13.

References

Fischel, William A.1989. "Did *Serrano* Cause Proposition 13?" *National Tax Journal* 42: 465-74.

———. 1996. "How *Serrano* Caused Proposition 13." *Journal of Law and Politics* 12: 607-45.

———. 2004. "Did John Serrano Vote for Proposition 13? A Reply to Stark and Zasloff, 'Tiebout and Tax Revolts: Did *Serrano <u>Really</u>* Cause Proposition 13?'" *UCLA Law Review* 51: 887-932.

———. 2008. "*Serrano* and Proposition 13: Comment on Isaac Martin, "Does School Finance Litigation Cause Taxpayer Revolt." Working paper, Dartmouth College Economics Department.

Martin, Isaac. 2006. "Does School Finance Litigation Cause Taxpayer Revolt? *Serrano* and Proposition 13." *Law and Society Review* 40: 525-57.

Sears, David O., and Jack Citrin. 1985. *Tax Revolt: Something for Nothing in California,* enlarged edition. Cambridge, Mass.: Harvard University Press.

Stark, Kirk, and Jonathan Zasloff. 2003. "Tiebout and Tax Revolts: Did *Serrano* Really Cause Proposition 13?" *UCLA Law Review* 50: 801-58.

Sunstein, Cass R. 2006. *Infotopia: How Many Minds Produce Knowledge.* New York: Oxford University Press.

Chapter 7

Proposition 13 and Residential Mobility

Terri A. Sexton[1]

Introduction

Proposition 13 transformed California's property tax from a market-value based tax to an acquisition-value based tax under which the assessed value of a property equals the market value at the time the property is sold, but can increase by no more than 2% per year until the next change in ownership. Acquisition value assessment discourages mobility because property owners lose their tax break from the assessment limit when they sell. Property taxes can rise dramatically after a move, even if the market value of the new property is the same or less than the old one. Young households may choose not to move to larger houses as their families grow in size and older households may not downsize as their children leave. Homeowners may not move if their job location changes and may not accept a job offer if it necessitates a move. Households may not "vote with their feet" by choosing to move to communities that provide their desired local services and taxes. These choices result in inefficient resource allocation and decreased economic welfare.

---

[1] Associate Director, CSLT, UCD; Professor of Economics, CSUS.

To illustrate this mobility or "lock-in" effect consider a California household that purchased a home in 1980 for $200,000. This home was assessed at $200,000 in 1980 (its market value at the time of purchase) and the tax bill was 1% of assessed value or $2,000. Twenty-five years later, in 2005, the same house, assuming it had experienced the average appreciation of residential property in California over this period (433%), was worth $1,065,700. However, under the provisions of Proposition 13, the property's assessed value could increase at most 2% per year provided the household had not sold it, so in 2005 this house had an assessed value of $328,121 and a tax bill of $3,281. Had the household elected to sell this house and purchase an identical (same value) home elsewhere in the state in 2005, they would have owed $10,657 in taxes on their new home, a difference of $7,376 or over $600 per month. Even if they chose to purchase a smaller home worth say $500,000, roughly half the value of their former home, they would face a tax increase of over $1,700 per year ($5,000-$3,281). These increased tax costs are not one-time penalties for moving but continue or persist year after year.

This chapter examines the theoretical nature of this mobility or lock-in effect and reviews the empirical evidence as to its magnitude. The next section summarizes theoretical and empirical studies of the determinants of household mobility, especially the role of transactions costs. Section 3 presents the empirical evidence of the lock-in effect of an acquisition value-based property tax and Section 4 discusses the consequences of reduced residential mobility. Finally Section 5 summarizes and concludes.

Household Mobility

The extensive literature on household mobility has identified many factors that influence the decision to relocate. In simplest terms, a household will change residence if their expected utility after the move is higher than their utility before the move and the increase in utility more than compensates for the costs of moving.

A move can be motivated by life-cycle events such as new household formation, marriage, birth of children, and aging. Typically, as individuals move through their life-cycle they experience changes in preferences, needs, and resources that influence their housing demand. Households also move to adjust the characteristics of their housing unit or neighborhood or to increase accessibility to their workplace, family and friends, and schools and shopping. For example anything that raises the time, cost, or frustration associated with commuting to work such as job relocation or higher gasoline prices may bring about a move. Quigley and Weinberg (1977), Weinberg (1979), and Weinberg, Friedman and Mayo (1981) explore the factors that precipitate a move.

Ultimately, the decision to move is based on a comparison between the expected gain in utility and the cost of achieving it, or transactions costs that can include search costs, realtor fees, mortgage interest and closing costs, moving costs, capital gains taxes, and *ad valorem* transfer and property taxes. These transactions costs, if large enough, can deter a household from moving. Empirical studies show that changes in housing consumption are slow in response to changes in desired consumption because of transactions costs. For example Weinberg, Friedman, and Mayo (1981) find that the costs of searching and moving have a significant impact on the mobility of low-income renter households.

The impact of the tax on capital gains arising from the sale of a home is the focus of several studies. Up until 1997, such gains were taxed if the seller did not go on to buy a more expensive home though if the homeowner was age 55 or older they qualified for a one-time exclusion of $125,000 of capital gains. This likely caused homeowners younger than 55 who wanted to trade down, to postpone such a move until age 55. The Taxpayer Relief Act of 1997 (TRA97) eliminated the differential treatment based on age and provided the data necessary to empirically measure the extent of the lock-in effect on under-55 homeowners.

Cunningham and Engelhardt (2008) utilize Current Population Survey data on homeowners just above (56-58 year-olds) and below (52-54 year-olds) the age-55 threshold, both before (1996) and after (1998) TRA97, to estimate the impact of removing the age threshold on the relative mobility of these two groups of homeowners. Using a difference-in-difference approach they find that eliminating the age threshold had a statistically significant affect on the mobility of under-55 homeowners, increasing their mobility by from 1.0 to 1.4 percentage points, or 22-31% of their mean mobility rate of 4%. Their results are consistent with the estimates of earlier studies that were based on more modest reforms (Newman and Reschovsky 1987; Sinai 1998)

Lundborg and Skedinger (1998) use changes in capital gains tax rules to estimate the lock-in effect of transaction costs in Sweden. They argue that transaction costs will reduce residential mobility if the homeowner is mismatched in the current residence and thus focus on households that have recently experienced changes in income or family size. They find that the capital gains tax reduces the probability of moving among mismatched households seeking to move to smaller homes. In particular, among households that experience a decrease in income and hence housing demand, a 1% increase in capital gains taxes is found to result in a 0.12 to 0.13% reduction in the probability of moving.

Like the capital gains tax, a real estate transfer tax is a one-time cost associated with selling (or buying) a home. This tax is essentially a sales tax on housing because it is a percentage of the sales price. Van Ommeren and Van Leuvensteijn (2005) measure the lock-in effect caused by a transfer tax in the Netherlands. The authors use a sample of over 16,000 Dutch households from the Income Panel Research (IPR) database. They demonstrate empirically that the 6% *ad valorem* transfer tax paid by buyers in the Netherlands has a strong negative effect on the owners' probability of moving. Specifically, they find that a 1 percentage point increase in the transfer tax decreases residential mobility rates by at least 8%.

Another factor that influences the homeowner's decision to sell their existing home and purchase another is the change in credit costs, namely the mortgage interest rate. If the household currently has a mortgage at a favorable rate (below the current rate) they may be reluctant to pay this off and borrow at the higher current rate. Doing so would involve a transaction cost that will impact them over the life of the mortgage. Quigley (1987) examines the decline in residential mobility caused by increases in mortgage interest rates. His empirical analysis indicates that the lock-in effect of favorable mortgage terms is quite large. According to his estimates, the average homeowner in 1981 would have lost $1,800 if its mortgage had been financed at 1981 rates and the difference in premium ranged from a low of zero for households who owned their homes free and clear to a high of $66,000 in 1981 when the average market value of houses in the sample was $45,000.

Mobility Effect of Acquisition-Value Based Property Taxes

A property tax system based on acquisition-value assessment results in a lock-in effect similar to that associated with the transactions costs discussed above. Property taxes can rise dramatically when a household purchases a new home, even if they pay less for the new home than they received for the old one, because the new home will be taxed based on market value. Rather than lose the benefit of a reduced assessment on their current home resulting from the limit, households may choose to postpone moving to an otherwise preferred residence. Unlike a transfer tax or capital gains tax, this added transaction or "moving" cost must be paid every year, making it more like having to pay a higher mortgage interest rate. However, unless assessments are frozen, the allowable percentage increase in assessed value will mean that each year the difference between the taxes on the original home and the new home will grow larger. Therefore it is expected that acquisition-value assessment should have a larger negative impact on household mobility than that found by Quigley (1987) in the case of rising interest rates.

In *Property Taxes and Tax Revolts*, O'Sullivan, Sheffrin, and I (1995a) explore the effects of an acquisition-value tax on the mobility of homeowners using a simple theoretical model of the costs and benefits of relocation. Our model incorporates property taxes into the household's optimization problem, allowing us to compare the optimum time per dwelling under a conventional property tax and an acquisition-value tax. Under both tax systems households increase the time between moves as moving costs increase. In the case of an acquisition-value tax, the optimum time per dwelling increases as the tax rate, the market value of the property, and the rate of appreciation of the property increase. Whenever property values grow faster than the assessment limit, the optimum time per dwelling will be larger under acquisition-value compared to market-value assessment.

We use a numerical (simulation) version of the model to compute the optimal time per dwelling under the two taxes. Assuming a 3% property tax rate, a 2% assessment cap, and 6% inflation in home values, the time per dwelling is always longer for the acquisition tax, by as much as 12% (10.47 years versus 9.31 years) for the least mobile households. A higher housing inflation rate of 13% results in a larger penalty for moving and an increase of as much as 26% in the time per dwelling under the acquisition- versus market-value tax.

Theoretically, an acquisition-value based property tax introduces moving penalties resulting in a lock-in effect, the magnitude of which depends on other features of the property tax system such as the tax rate and the assessment limit, and features of the housing market, namely housing prices and their rate of appreciation. Currently there are 14 states that limit the increase in the assessed value of homeowner property and apply an acquisition-value rule that resets assessed value to market value at the time of sale. These states are identified in Table 1. Assessment limits range from a low of 2% in California to as high as 10% in several states and over 16% in Montana. Several empirical studies have attempted to measure the lock-in effect resulting from acquisition-value assessment. While the majority of these have focused on California, others have looked at Florida and Georgia.

Nagy (1997) was among the first to analyze the impact of Proposition 13's impact on household mobility. He examined the short-run effects immediately before and after Proposition 13 was introduced by comparing mobility in three California Metropolitan Statistical Areas (San Bernardino, San Diego, and San Francisco) and seven areas outside the state (Cincinnati, Columbus, Kansas City, New Orleans, Philadelphia, Rochester, and San Antonio). He used data from the U.S. Census Bureau's 1975, 1978, and 1982 Annual Housing Surveys, which allowed him to calculate and compare homeowner duration in the pre- and post-Proposition 13 periods. Nagy's results indicate that households experienced significantly longer average housing tenure after 1978, but this was true for both California and non-California households. In fact, San Francisco's decline in mobility was significantly greater than only that of Philadelphia. He argues that rising mortgage rates over this period (from an average of 9.0% between 1975 and 1977 to 12.6% between 1978 and 1982) likely caused a general decline in mobility nationwide as suggested by Quigley (1987).

The time period analyzed by Nagy may have been too short to measure the mobility effect of Proposition 13. The moving penalty associated with acquisition value assessment grows over time as the gap between market value and assessed value of the property increases. In fact, as he points out, in the year or two following passage of Proposition 13 homeowners may have had an incentive to sell their homes sooner so as to establish a new base year assessment in their new homes.

Stohs, Childs, and Stevenson (2001) examine the longer-term effects of Proposition 13 on mobility by comparing housing sales in California to those in Illinois and Massachusetts from 1995 to 2000. They measure mobility as the percentage of homes sold per year and compare this across census tracts in Or-

Table 1. States with Acquisition Value Assessment

State	Coverage	Eligible Property	Limit	Tax-Rate Limits
Arkansas	Statewide (constitutional)	All	Homestead 5%, other 10%	X
California	Statewide (constitutional)	All	Lesser of 2% or inflation	X
District of Columbia	Districtwide	Homestead	10%; 5% for qualifying low income	X
Florida	Statewide (constitutional)	Homestead	Lesser of 3% or inflation	X
Georgia	Local option (local constitutional)	Homestead	Freeze (0%)	X
Illinois	Local option	Homestead	7% with maximum exemption value of $33,000	X

State	Jurisdiction	Property type	Limit	
Maryland	Statewide	Homestead	10% statewide for state taxes; local options for local taxes range from 0% to 10%	X
Michigan	Statewide (constitutional)	All	Lesser of 5% or inflation	X
Montana	Statewide	All	16.66%/yr phase-in of reassessment over 6 yrs	X
New Mexico	Statewide	Residential	0.03	X
New York	New York City & Nassau County	Residential with 10 or fewer units	6% (residential up to three units) or 8% (other residential) per year; 20% or 30% over 5 years	X
Oklahoma	Statewide (constitutional)	All	0.05	X
South Carolina	Statewide (constitutional)	Homestead	15% over 5 years	X
Texas	Statewide (constitutional)	Homestead	0.1	X

Sources: Anderson (2006), Haveman and Sexton (2008).

ange and Sacramento Counties in California, Dupage County, Illinois, and areas of Boston, Massachusetts. They find substantially less movement in California with an average percentage of homes sold over the 1995-2000 period of 5.7% in California, 6.3% in Massachusetts, and 8.1% in Illinois. They then translate these into average years spent per dwelling of 17.5, 15.9, and 12.3 years respectively. Both regression analysis and statistical tests of the differences in means across states support their hypothesis that mobility was significantly lower in California.

A key argument used to garner support for Proposition 13 was that senior citizens were being forced to sell their homes because they could not afford their rapidly rising property taxes. By the mid-1980s this argument had completely reversed; senior citizens could not afford to sell their homes because they could not afford the increased property taxes on new, though smaller homes. To address this new concern, Proposition 60 (1986) allowed persons over age 55 to transfer the assessed value of their homes to a replacement dwelling of equal or lesser value in the same county without a change of ownership reassessment. This exemption is available only once in a lifetime and it was expanded in 1988 (Proposition 90) to allow senior homeowners to transfer their assessed value to a comparable dwelling in a different county if the receiving county agrees. Together, these measures essentially remove the lock-in effect after age 55.

This portability feature provides a unique perspective from which to examine the mobility effects associated with an acquisition value property tax. If the tax benefit from Proposition 13 affects household decisions to move, a significant increase in mobility rates for homeowners aged 55 or older should be observed. Ferreria (2004) uses the Integrated Public Use Microdata Series (IPUMS) to compare the mobility of 55-year olds to 54-year olds in 1980 and 1990. He finds that in 1990 the probability of moving among California 55-year olds is from 1.2 to 1.5 percentage points higher when compared to 54-year olds, representing an increase of approximately 25% on a base of 4%. No such differences are found among other control groups including 1990 renters in California, 1990 homeowners in Texas, and 1980 homeowners in California.

Our theoretical model and simulation results (O'Sullivan, Sexton, and Sheffrin 1995a) show that the lock-in effect of an acquisition-value tax should increase with housing prices and the rate of appreciation in housing prices. Wasi and White (2005) confirm this hypothesis in their empirical comparison of California homeowner mobility to that of Texas and Florida from 1970 to 2000. Using IPUMS data and a difference-in-difference approach, they conclude that the average ownership tenure for California households was 0.66 years or 6% longer than households in Texas and Florida and 6% longer than the average tenure of California owners in 1970. They also find that the responses to Proposition 13 have varied considerably across California. Specifically, according to their results, the average tenure of homeowners increased 0.64 years in Fresno and Riverside where housing prices and housing price appreciation are lower, 1.2 years in Los Angeles/Orange County, and from two to more than three years in the coastal areas of San Francisco, Santa Barbara, and San Jose where housing prices and appreciation are among the highest in the state.

All of the empirical studies that have sought to measure the magnitude of the lock-in effect of Proposition 13 at least 10 years after its passage have concluded that the effect exists and is significant. However, there is variation in the estimated magnitude of the effect and it is difficult to compare results because they differ in the way the effect is measured and the data and methods used to estimate it.

California is not the only state with an acquisition-value property tax (see Table 1) though only two studies have estimated the lock-in effect in other states. Muscogee County, Georgia, adopted a true acquisition-value property tax system in 1983 under which the assessed value of homesteaded property is frozen for local property tax purposes. Sjoquist and Pandey (2001) examined 1997 residential sales to determine if the assessment freeze created a lock-in effect for Muscogee County homeowners. For every homesteaded property, the county must maintain two values, the acquisition (frozen) value for local tax purposes and the market value for state taxes. If the assessment freeze creates a lock-in effect then the probability of a house selling should be negatively related to the benefit of the freeze, namely the difference between the market value and the frozen value.

Sjoquist and Pandey estimate a probit regression model in which the dependent variable equals one if the house sold in 1997 and zero otherwise. Independent variables include the benefit of the freeze measured as the absolute or percentage difference between market value and frozen assessed value, a set of dummy variables to measure the number of years that the homeowner has occupied the house, and a set of socio-economic control variables measured at the census tract level. They find that the benefit of the freeze is not statistically significant in explaining the probability of moving, leading to their conclusion that the assessment limit has no significant impact on housing turnover or household mobility in Georgia.

Stansel, Jackson, and Finch (2007) came to a similar conclusion with respect to Florida's "Save Our Homes" assessment cap that limits increases in residential homestead assessed values to 3% per year until the home is sold. They examine the average tenure of homeowners in 20 Florida counties in two different years, 2002 and 2006. Using county tax roll data, they calculate how many years the existing owner of each homesteaded property has owned that property and then compute that average, median, and standard deviation for each county. They find that average tenure actually declined from 11.20 years in 2002 to 10.83 years in 2006 with lower average tenure and larger decreases between 2002 and 2006 in coastal counties.

The authors acknowledge that these results contradict expectations and offer several possible explanations. A large volume of new construction in response to rapid population growth will tend to reduce average tenure. The authors found that when they omit all properties built after 2002, average tenure did increase slightly from 11.20 years in 2002 to 11.44 years in 2006. Rapidly rising housing prices may also have contributed to reduced tenure by increasing home sales including speculative home purchases. Low mortgage-interest rates over this period may have also increased home sales, especially for first-time homebuyers, which in turn, would decrease average tenure. Finally, since the period of study was seven years after the assessment law went into effect it may be that homeowners had already adjusted their housing consumption so that no further differences in housing tenure could be observed.

Concern that the lock-in effect of Florida's assessment limit has trapped homeowners in their current residences remains and led to the approval of a portability measure in January 2008. Amendment 1 allows full-time Florida homeowners to take the tax benefits of their Save Our Homes assessment limit with them when they move. Specifically, they can transfer up to $500,000 of their assessed value savings on their old house and apply it to the assessed value of their new home. Observation of the impact of this amendment on home sales will provide another opportunity to estimate the mobility effect of the Save Our Homes assessment limit in Florida.

Consequences of the Lock-in Effect

The distortions of household mobility resulting from acquisition-value property tax systems can impede the efficient allocation of resources. Among the consequences addressed in previous studies are the negative welfare effects of suboptimal housing consumption (O'Sullivan, Sexton, and Sheffrin, 1995b), and reduced job mobility and increased unemployment (Van Ommeren, Rietveld, and Nijkamp, 2000). Other likely effects include increased commutes and a reduced stock of entry level housing. On the positive side, reduced household mobility promotes neighborhood stability, an argument used by the U.S. Supreme Court in its judgment in *Nordlinger* v. *Hahn* (U.S. Law Week, 60 LW 4563-4574) which upheld the constitutionality of Proposition 13.

As part of our extensive analysis of the impacts of Proposition 13 in the early 1990s (O'Sullivan, Sexton, and Sheffrin, 1995b), we used a simulation model to estimate the excess burden (loss in economic well-being) resulting from a switch from a conventional property tax to an acquisition-value tax. The excess burden incurred by a particular household as a result of the switch is the compensating variation or lump-sum payment required to restore the utility level achieved under a market-value system. The total excess burden is the sum of the compensating variations (some of which may be negative) across households. Assuming a 3% tax rate and property value appreciation of 6%, our results suggest that a revenue-neutral switch from a market-value to an acquisition-value system would result in an estimated annual compensating variation for the median household of $440 per year, representing about 4.5% of market-value tax liability or 0.88% of income. The excess burden increases with both the appreciation rate of housing and the tax rate.

Van Ommeren, Rietveld, and Nijkamp (2000) develop a theoretical search model to analyze the relationship between residential mobility, job mobility, and commuting. In their model the decisions to change residence and change jobs both involve a change in commuting distance and thus are mutually dependent. One of their main conclusions is that residential moving costs discourage unemployed persons from moving, decreasing the probability of becoming employed and increasing the number of unemployed persons. In some cases, moving costs can also discourage employed persons from changing jobs. An increase in the transaction cost of changing residences decreases residential mobility, increasing the commuting cost of changing jobs, reducing job mobility and possibly leading to increased unemployment. Their search model is consistent with the observation that a change of job that increases commuting distance normally triggers a residential move. However, if moving costs are sufficiently high, either the new job will not be accepted or the subsequent residential move may not occur.

These results suggest that transaction costs can be a deterrent to households moving when their job location changes, thereby increasing commuting distances and costs. Although no empirical tests have been performed, observed changes in commuting patterns in major metropolitan areas in California support this hypothesis. In particular, between 1980 and 1990, the number of workers in San Diego, San Francisco, and Los Angeles that commute outside the Metropolitan Statistical Area to work increased 119%, 88%, and 80% respectively. This is well above the growth in the number of such commuters in other metropolitan areas across the country that generally ranged from 25 to 45%. Figure 1 illustrates this comparison. Not only did the absolute number of outside-MSA commuters increase faster in California but the percentage of the workforce making these commutes also increased at a faster rate in California. While these census data are consistent with the conclusion that the moving penalty resulting from California's acquisition-value property tax has increased commutes, more research is needed to determine the extent to which Proposition 13 has contributed to this increase.

Other consequences of the lock-in effect of Proposition 13 have also been observed but not tested. They include potential impacts on the stock of housing. When households face a moving penalty, one possible response is to alter their existing residence to make it more nearly resemble what they would choose if they did not face high moving costs. If a household chooses to add square footage to their existing home, they maintain the benefit of a lower assessment on the original square footage while only the added square footage is taxed at its current market value, usually the cost of construction. Thus we have seen two- and three-bedroom homes transformed into three- and four-bedroom homes respectively. In this way, the stock of available "entry-level" housing has diminished.

Despite these consequences, all of which were pointed out by the critics of Proposition 13 in the years following its passage, the U.S. Supreme Court in its majority opinion argued that the assessment provisions of Proposition 13 fur-

Figure 1. Change in Commuters from Within to Outside Metro Areas: 1980 to 1990

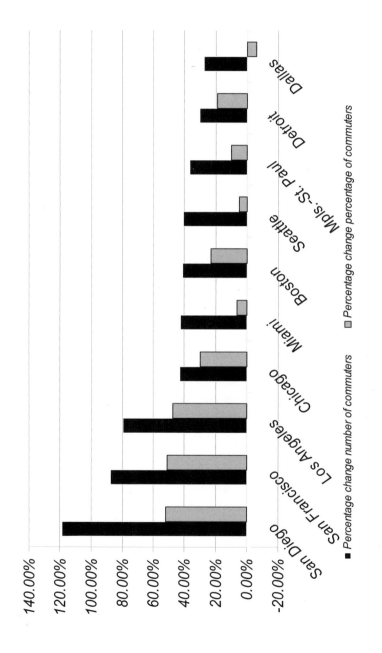

■ Percentage change number of commuters
▨ Percentage change percentage of commuters

thered the state interest in local neighborhood preservation, continuity, and stability. Thus the moving penalty was regarded as a virtue, albeit one that was never mentioned by supporters of Proposition 13 either before or after its passage.

Summary and Conclusions

Empirical studies confirm that households respond to increased transactions costs by not adjusting their housing consumption as often as they would in the absence of such costs, thereby reducing their mobility and introducing inefficiencies in housing markets. In the case of acquisition-value taxes, however, the empirical evidence is mixed. In California the consensus has been that Proposition 13 has had a significant negative effect on mobility. However, the estimates of its magnitude vary from study to study and are shown to vary over time and geographically across the state. In the two other states that have been studied, Florida and Georgia, the empirical evidence suggests that the lock-in effect, if it exists, is not significant.

The efficiency consequences of reduced household mobility include the excess burden on households from suboptimal housing consumption, inefficient labor market outcomes, longer commutes with associated environmental and congestion costs, a reduction in the supply of smaller homes for young and old homebuyers, and reduced incentives for households to vote with their feet, thereby impeding the efficient provision of local public goods.

Theory suggests that an acquisition-value property tax imposes a moving penalty similar to other costs associated with selling one home and moving to another such as higher mortgage interest costs, capital gains taxes, and real estate transfer taxes. However, more research is needed to ascertain the magnitude of the moving penalty and its associated efficiency costs.

References

Anderson, Nathan B. 2006. "Property Tax Limitations: An Interpretative Review." *National Tax Journal* 59(3): 685-94.

Cunningham, Christopher R., and Gary V. Engelhardt. 2008. "Housing Capital-Gains Taxation and Homeowner Mobility: Evidence from the Taxpayer Relief Act of 1997." *Journal of Urban Economics* 63:803-15.

Ferreira, Fernando. 2004. "You Can Take It with You: Transferability of Proposition 13 Tax Benefits, Residential Mobility, and Willingness to Pay for Housing Amenities." Working Paper 72. Berkeley: Center for Labor Economics, University of California.

Haveman, Mark, and Terri A. Sexton. 2008. *Property Tax Assessment Limits: Lessons from Thirty Years of Experience.* Cambridge, Mass.: Lincoln Institute of Land Policy, Policy Focus Report.

Lundborg, Per, and Per Skedinger. 1998. "Capital Gains Taxation and Residential Mobility in Sweden." *Journal of Public Economics* 67:399-419.

Nagy, John. 1997. "Did Proposition 13 Affect the Mobility of California Homeowners?" *Public Finance Review* 25(1): 102-15.

Newman, S., and J. Reschovsky. 1987. "An Evaluation of the One-Time Capital Gains Exclusion for Older Homeowners" *American Real Estate and Urban Economics Association Journal* 15:704-24.

O'Sullivan, Arthur, Terri A. Sexton, and Steven M. Sheffrin. 1995a. *Property Taxes & Tax Revolts.* New York: Cambridge University Press.

———. 1995b. "Property Taxes, Mobility, and Home Ownership." *Journal of Urban Economics* 37:107-29.

Quigley, John M. 1987. "Interest Rate Variations, Mortgage Prepayments and Household Mobility." *Review of Economics and Statistics* 69(4): 636-43.

Quigley, John, and Daniel Weinberg. 1977. "The Determinants of Intra-Urban Household Mobility: A Review and Synthesis." *International Regional Science Review* 2:41-46.

Sinai, T. 1998. "Taxation, User Cost, and Household Mobility Decisions." Working Paper no. 303. Wharton School, University of Pennsylvania.

Sjoquist, David L., and Lakshmi Pandey. 2001. "An Analysis of Acquisition Value Property Tax Assessment for Homesteaded Property." *Public Budgeting and Finance* (winter): 1-17.

Stansel, Dean, Gary Jackson, and J. Howard Finch. 2007. "Housing Tenure and Mobility with an Acquisition-Based Property Tax: The case of Florida." *Journal of Housing Research* 16(2): 117-29.

Stohs, Mark Hoven, Paul Childs, and Simon Stevenson. 2001. "Tax Policies and Residential Mobility." *International Real Estate Review* 4(1): 95-117.

Van Ommeren, Jos, and Michiel Van Leuvensteijn. 2005. "New Evidence of the Effect of Transaction Costs on Residential Mobility." *Journal of Regional Science* 45(4): 681-702.

Van Ommeren, Jos N., Piet Rietveld, and Peter Nijkamp. 2000. "Job Mobility, Residential Mobility, and Commuting: A Theoretical Analysis Using Search Theory." *Annals of Regional Science* 34:13-32.

Wasi, Nada, and Michelle J. White. 2005. "Property Tax Limitations and Mobility: Lock-in Effect of California's Proposition 13." *Brookings-Wharton Papers on Urban Affairs*: 59-88.

Weinberg, Daniel. 1979. "The Determinants of Intra-Urban Mobility." *Regional Science and Urban Economics* 9:219-46.

Weinberg, Daniel H., Joseph Friedman, and Stephen K. Mayo. 1981. "Intra-Urban Residential Mobility: The Role of Transaction Costs, Market Imperfections, and Household Disequilibrium." *Journal of Urban Economics* 9:332-48.

Chapter 8

Rethinking the Fairness of Proposition 13

Steven M. Sheffrin[1]

Thirty years after its enactment, Proposition 13 still remains emblematic both in terms of its significance as a fiscal innovation, but also in its iconic unfairness. Defenders of Proposition 13, of course, recognize its potential unfairness in terms of horizontal equity—that property owners with identical houses in the very same jurisdiction may have radically differing tax burdens—but justify it by the longer term benefits they believe that Proposition 13 has delivered for all homeowners.

Property taxation, however, has evolved in the United States, in part driven by Proposition 13 and other measures throughout the country that it inspired. In particular, tax limitations are now ubiquitous, and Proposition 13 represents just one of the many flavors of property tax limitations. This suggests that it is time to rethink the fairness of Proposition 13 in the broader context of the U.S. property tax experience and not just highlight aspects of Proposition 13 in isolation.

This chapter undertakes such a re-examination. I first begin by reviewing the empirical evidence on horizontal inequities generated by Proposition 13's assessment system and offer some projections for the future. I then present an

[1] Professor of Economics, Department of Economics, UC Davis. Support for this research was provided by the Center for State and Local Taxation at UC Davis.

argument offered in defense of the fairness of Proposition 13 in terms of an equitable intertemporal steady state, as well as review the United States Supreme Court's own thinking on the matter. Stepping back, I explore the public perception of the implicit alternative to Proposition 13 in most discussions—unfettered market value property taxation. Drawing on a variety of sources, I explain why the public has rejected this alternative as a normative model. I then return to Proposition 13 in this new light for some suggestions for reform.

Proposition 13 and Horizontal Inequities

To understand the horizontal inequities generated by Proposition 13, it is necessary to review its basic provisions and introduce some terminology. When Proposition 13 was passed in 1978, assessments of property were rolled back to the levels that prevailed in 1975. In each subsequent year, the assessed value of a property could increase by a maximum of 2% until the property was sold, at which time it was assessed at its market value. The year in which a property is sold is known as the *base year*. Properties that were last sold before 1975 are assigned 1975 base years. Finally, if properties are substantially modified but not sold, the new portion of the property is assessed at market value, while the pre-existing part retains its prior assessment.

Horizontal inequities are typically measured by the *disparity ratio*—the ratio of market to assessed value. The disparity ratio will vary by base year, with properties with older base years having the largest disparity ratios. Modified properties will have lower disparity ratios because they are effectively combinations of newly assessed property and property with older base years.

Work by O'Sullivan, Sexton, and Sheffrin (1995) and updated in Sheffrin and Sexton (1998) provides in-depth analysis of the horizontal inequities generated by Proposition 13. Table 1, drawn from this work, examines the disparity ratios for 1975 and percentage of properties in this class both for single-family homeowner properties and commercial and industrial properties in Los Angeles County. I focus on the disparity ratios for these years because they are the most extreme. In areas that grew rapidly in the 1980s and 1990s, such as the counties west of Los Angeles—Riverside and San Bernardino—and the Central Valley, the overall disparities are considerably less because a higher proportion of the properties have more recent base years.

To understand the table, consider the first row for nonmodified single-family homeowners in Los Angeles. In 1991, the 1975 disparity ratio was 5.19, which was the ratio of current market value to the assessed value for a home with a 1975 base year. In 1991, 43% of all the properties in this class had a 1975 base year. By 1996, a drop in housing prices had brought down the disparity ratio to 3.84 and properties with a 1975 base year accounted for only 33% of non-modified properties due to new construction and sales. The second row presents the data for modified properties. Note, as expected, that the disparity ratios are less. However, since modifying a property is an alternative to selling it, the

Table 1. Disparities in Los Angeles County

Class of Property	Modified	1991 Disparity Ratio 1975 median	1991 1975 Base Year %	1996 Disparity Ratio 1975 median	1996 1975 Base Year %
Single Family Owner	No	5.19	43	3.84	33
Single Family Owner	Yes	4.35	47	3.24	43
Commercial and Industrial	No	5.66	36	3.23	29
Commercial and Industrial	Yes	4.19	45	2.34	43

decrease in 1975 base year properties between 1991 and 1996 is considerably less than for nonmodified properties.

Disparities for later base years are much smaller. In fact, in 1996, non-modified homeowner property in Los Angeles with base years of 1988 or later had disparity ratios of approximately 1.0. These properties accounted for 43% of all nonmodified homeowner property. For this large segment of properties, there were effectively no disparities whatsoever.

The table also presents data for commercial and industrial properties in Los Angeles. Again, note that the disparity ratios are lower for modified commercial properties but their turnover is also low. Modified commercial and industrial properties are much larger in assessed and market value than unmodified properties.

Using Case-Shiller housing price indices for Los Angeles, I can provide updated estimates of the 1975 disparity ratios for homeowners through 2008. Starting with the value of disparity ratio for unmodified properties of 3.84, I adjust this figure using housing price increases and allowing for a yearly maximum of 2% adjustment in assessed value. Figure 1 presents estimates of the disparities for the 1975 base year properties as well as estimates for 1988 base year properties (which had a disparity ratio of 1.0 in 1996).

As the figure depicts, the housing boom through 2005 drove up prices and disparity ratios, with 1975 base year properties' disparities peaking over 11 before dropping to approximately 8 in 2008. For 1988 base year properties, disparities rose from one to nearly three before dropping back to approximately two. Properties purchased after 1988 would have lower disparities.

Figure 1. Estimates of Disparity Ratios for Los Angeles Homeowners

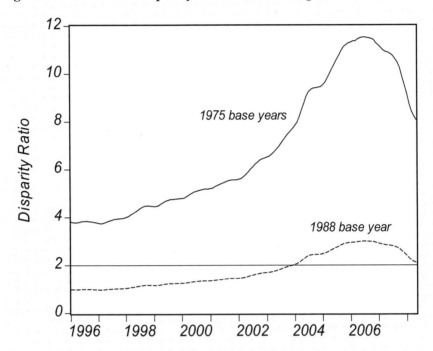

Clearly, the inequities generated by Proposition 13 are much greater for the 1975 base year properties. Sheffrin and Sexton (1998) estimate that the 1975 base year properties would fall below 15% for homeowners by 2016, based on turnover projections. Substantial 1975 base year percentages would only remain for large, modified commercial and industrial properties.

The ups and downs of the real estate market also have affects on other aspects of taxpayer equity. Sheffrin and Sexton (1988) document that during the housing crash in the early 1990s more wealthy areas suffered the most. Table 2 presents estimates of disparity ratios for two locations in Los Angeles for 1991 and 1996, the up-scale Santa Monica area and the less affluent West Covina. The disparity ratio in Santa Monica fell from 7.0 to 4.3 over that period, while in West Covina the decline was more modest, from 4.9 to 3.8. Housing recessions promote equality.

Using data on homeowners matched to income tax records for 1991, O'Sullivan, Sheffrin, and Sexton (1995) explored the equity aspects of Proposition 13 in more detail. One way to evaluate the equity of Proposition 13's assessment system would be to consider a revenue neutral change to a market

Table 2. Housing Price Declines In Los Angeles County Reduced Inequalities

Year	1991 1975 Disparity Ratio	1996 1975 Disparity Ratio	Average Assessed Value 1996
Region			
West Covina	4.9	3.8	$45,778
Santa Monica	7.0	4.3	$124,734

value system, in which all assessments would be raised to market value but rates lowered within a county to keep total revenues constant. A revenue neutral switch to a market value system would disadvantage lower-income homeowners and seniors over the age of 65. Lower-income homeowners move less frequently than higher-income homeowners and thus would lose more of the benefits from Proposition 13. Seniors are disproportionately concentrated in 1975 base years properties and would be big losers as well. In fact, over 82% of seniors in Los Angeles would have been worse off under a switch to a revenue neutral market value property tax.

Although these thought experiments are useful, evaluating the equity of Proposition 13 is difficult for two reasons. First, within each income or age class, there is still considerable horizontal inequity—some higher income home-owners move frequently while others do not. Second, Proposition 13 also lowered total property tax collections and other taxes or charges were substituted for property taxes. Those taxes, in turn, create their own burdens which may vary by income class or age.

Could Proposition 13 Be Fair?

Under certain conditions, a property tax system based on acquisition values like Proposition 13 could replicate a market value system over the life time of property owners. Consider the following scenario: all homeowners live in identical homes for a fixed number of years (e.g., seven) before moving to a new residence, the nominal rate of property appreciation is constant, and the property tax rate is constant. Initially, assume for these homeowners that the times since their last sale are evenly dispersed over the seven-year holding period. The government raises a constant amount of real revenue each period.

An outside observer, who took a snapshot of the situation but was not privy to the underlying dynamics, would view this situation as highly unequal. At any point in time, market and assessed value would differ and those individuals who were in the properties the longest would have the largest gaps. New homeowners would appear to be disproportionately funding the government. However, over the lifetime of homeowners, they would all enjoy the same benefits and privileges of the acquisition value system. Every seven years they would move and the value of their assessments brought back to market value. Since the homeowners are situated equally over their lifetimes, their lifetime shares of financing the government are constant—although their payments in any one year will differ depending on where they are in the residential mobility cycle.

This argument is revealing a number of different ways. It does shows Proposition 13 does need to be evaluated from an intertemporal perspective. But it also demonstrates the strict conditions necessary to generate intertemporal fairness. As a practical matter, households differ sharply in their mobility patterns and choice of home size, and housing prices rise (and fall) at different rates over time. These deviations from the proposed scenario generate intertemporal inequalities. In addition, contrary to the hypothetical scenario, in reality it has taken a long time for the initial benefits granted by Proposition 13—the 1975 base years—to work their way through the system and they have yet to fully disappear.

Perhaps more important, though, is that the intuition behind the intertemporal argument suggests a source of psychological support for Proposition 13. Purchasers of new homes are well aware that they pay more in property taxes than some of their neighbors. Yet, they also know that over time they will become "those neighbors" and enjoy the longer term benefits of Proposition 13. New purchasers are not searching for mathematical equivalence, but a sense that they will receive predictable benefits in the long run.

The United States Supreme Court upheld Proposition 13 from legal challenge on equal protection grounds. Did they believe it was fair or equitable? For matters in the sphere of economics or public finance, the Court used the relatively weak "rational basis" test under Equal Protection Clause to justify legal distinctions. The Court asks simply if there can be, in principle, any rational basis for the distinction being made, even if this was not explicit legislative intent. In *Nordlinger v. Hahn* (505 U.S. 1 [1992]), the majority opinion believed that a rational argument could be made for Proposition 13 and highlighted its potential to preserve neighborhoods by reducing homeowner mobility. However, the Court needed to distinguish its ruling in this case from a prior ruling in *Allegheny Pittsburgh Coal Co. v. County Commission* (448 U.S. 336 [1989]) in which the Court found that a property tax system in West Virginia, in which an assessor made major revaluations of properties only upon sale, was unconstitutional. How did this differ from Proposition 13? According to Wood (2006), the Supreme Court distinguishes between substantive and systemic horizontal equity. Substantive horizontal equity bases comparisons of taxpayers relative to their income or wealth and mirrors the use by economists of the concept. Systemic horizontal equity, on the other hand, focuses on the consistency, regularity, and certainty of application. The courts have been most concerned with fair procedure, not fair outcomes as measured by an objective standard.

In California, the assessment provisions had been adopted by the voters and enshrined in the state constitution, whereas in West Virginia, state law called for uniform assessment at market value but the practice of the local assessor was to base assessment primarily on acquisition value. Similar taxpayers in West Virginia were, therefore, potentially subject to arbitrary and capricious treatment—this was a violation of "systemic" horizontal equity. The Court was sensitive to these violations in West Virginia, but was willing to allow the substantive horizontal inequities in assessments in California to continue. Using this approach, Proposition 13 was fair enough to meet constitutional standards.

Another reason why the U.S. Supreme Court was reluctant to address substantive inequities in property taxes is because inequities are common in property tax systems across the states even those that officially embrace market value taxation. Many states have infrequent assessment cycles, with the result that market and assessed values can differ widely, for example, across classes of property or by the time since the last recorded sale. At times of rapidly changing properties prices, these divergences between market and assessed values can become quite large. The Court did not want to play the role of assessor-in-chief for the entire United States.

Public Perceptions of Market Value Property Taxation

Economists and tax policy theorists have great respect and admiration for a system of local market value property taxes, both on grounds of efficiency and fairness. Oates (1999) provides a clear statement of these views. A system of local property taxes allows homeowners to "vote with their feet" and move to neighborhoods to provide the packages of services and taxes they desire. Competition between jurisdictions can promote governmental efficiency. This is the "benefit" view of property taxation. Moreover, since land—a major component of the property tax base—is not mobile, there are limited economic distortions from imposing the tax. Fairness can be seen in two different lights. From the mobility perspective, homeowners are choosing what they want—just like they choose consumer goods. Moreover, since land and property ownership increases with income, the property tax can be seen as a relatively progressive tax. This is the "wealth" view of property taxation. Not all analysts share this sanguine perspective and Zodrow (2006) highlights many of its difficulties. Nonetheless systems of market value property taxation are generally held in favorable light by theoretically oriented scholars and policymakers.

These views, however, are not shared by the public at large. Public opinion is notoriously harsh on the property tax. For example, the Tax Foundation's *2006 Annual Survey of U.S. Attitudes on Tax and Wealth* found that 39% of respondents characterized the property tax as "the worst tax—that is, least fair" of state and local taxes, compared to 20% for state income taxes, 18% for sales taxation, and 7% for the state corporate income tax. Only in 2007 as gasoline prices began to rise did the public find a tax—the gasoline tax—that they liked less than the property tax.

Taxpayers put this dislike of the property tax into action by enacting a variety of ingenious limits on property taxation. According to Anderson (2007), in 2006 only 5 of the 48 states of the continental United States had no limits. Not just in California but in Florida and other locales, the voters have rejected market value systems for acquisition systems that break the link between market and assessed values. Why is there this disconnect between elite opinion and public opinion?

In some respects, the folk wisdom of the public may be wiser than elite opinion. As a benefit tax in most states, the property tax system does not work very effectively. Virtually all states maintain some control over local educational spending and redistribute resources across districts through a variety of tax and subsidy schema. Thus, taxpayers cannot simply shop for districts with the educational package they desire without being affected by state redistribution mechanisms. In the extreme case, the state could dictate virtual equality in per pupil spending across districts—as mandated in California by the *Serrano* court decisions—thereby sharply reducing taxpayer options for districts with widely different levels of educational spending. Taxpayers may still sort by peer groups and use more limited fiscal means to achieve desired outcomes, but state restrictions do undercut the benefit rationale for the property tax.

Taxpayers are also rightly skeptical of role of the property tax as a wealth tax. In its earliest days in the late nineteenth century, the property tax did aspire to a universal tax on wealth, but a variety of practical difficulties soon restricted the tax to real and personal property. As a result, the property tax does not reach financial wealth and thus serves as a very imperfect means to tax assets. In general, as Campbell (2008) discusses, Americans have limited taste for redistribution. In surveys they may support general statements that the rich should pay more, but they oppose confiscatory taxation at high levels of income. Taxpayers are also reluctant to tax the wealthy too heavily. Attitudes towards the estate and gift tax are notoriously unfavorable.

What taxpayers really dislike, however, about the property tax is their potential exposure to risk. Consider a local government collecting a fixed amount of property tax revenue to provide local services. The revenue received from each property is the tax rate times its assessed value. The tax rate adjusts to meet the preset revenue target. In this case, taxes on any given property depend on its *relative* share of total assessed value. Thus, any increase in the relative share will increase taxes.

Here are a few external events that could increase the property tax bill for a given homeowner:

- A new mall opens outside the community reducing the market value (and assessed value) of the mall within the community.
- A raft of foreclosures hit another part of the community with resulting property tax delinquencies and nonpayment.
- The EPA discloses that toxic wastes were found in another part of the community, sharply lowering market and assessed values.

- An assessor recalibrates his statistical assessment model and, based on recent sales of cul-de-sac property similar to that of the homeowner, increases the assessed value of the property more than the average for the community.
- Newly made entrepreneurs move into the neighborhood, which has the consequences of increasing the market and assessed value of the property.

All these events are outside the taxpayer's direct control and make the actual property tax bill risky for the taxpayers. Quoting from Adam Smith, Anderson (2007, p. 100), suggests that taxpayers may be guided by the principle that

> The tax each individual is bound to pay ought to be certain, and not arbitrary. . . . The certainty of what each individual ought to pay is, in taxation, a matter of so great importance, that a very considerable degree of inequality, it appears, I believe, from the experience of all nations is not near so great an evil as a very small degree of uncertainty.

The perceived unfairness of shifts in assessed values altering property tax payments may have deep psychological roots. Lind and Tyler (1988) proved a comprehensive review of a literature in social psychology that focuses on "procedural justice." In this tradition, procedures or processes that are perceived to be fair are those in which individuals affected by the decisions have a "voice" in the process. Voice can be effective by giving individuals a chance to alter outcomes and by also providing for opportunities for personal satisfaction from participation in the process or simple expression of their views.

At first glance, property taxes may fare well on this criterion. In the idealized New England style town-hall setting, local control of property tax rates, with decisions made by local governing boards, can be seen as example of permitting "voice" in the process of determining property tax payments. This is a natural complement to the "exit" alternative highlighted in the benefit view of taxation where taxpayers choose communities.

However, procedural justice is not met in property tax systems in which a property's tax bill is directly tied to its relative assessed value. What was striking about the events that could have impacted our hypothetical homeowner's relative share of market value was how abstract and distant they were from his or her immediate universe. The assessor did not pay a visit to and discuss whether the extensive new remodeling in kitchen and porch area warranted reassessment. Instead, assessments increased because of market forces outside the owner's control, newly uncovered knowledge, or perhaps worst of all, the vagaries of an impenetrable computer program. To the typical taxpayer it seems unfair that property tax bills can change, often dramatically, with potentially no change in actual value of a house or in the services provided by the community.

Other psychological factors are at work as well. Psychological researchers have long noted that individuals view personal belongings as extensions of themselves, value them in that light and, according to "symbolic self-completion theory" use them to communicate their identities to others. Recent research by Ledgerwood et al. (2007) demonstrates that the actual dollar values that indi-

viduals place on property also depend on social phenomena, such as group iden-
tity. Thus, valuations of property may be sensitive to social aspects of their environment that may not be directly correlated to economic phenomenon. For example, an influx of immigrants to a neighborhood could actually have a positive
influence on property values, but could be perceived negatively if the influx of
immigrants were viewed as a "threat" to the neighborhood.

Taxpayers respond to the uncertainty in their taxing environment by imposing limits on changes in tax assessments. Indeed, Anderson (2007) conjectures
that this flight from uncertainty may underlie taxpayer support for property tax
limitations. Proposition 13 may be an extreme case, but it is not an isolated phenomenon.

Proposition 13 in Historical Context

To place the origins of Proposition 13 in context, it is useful to develop two
ideal-types for property tax systems. Under a *budget-based system*, property tax
rates are adjusted to meet budgetary targets. Increases in assessed values are
offset by changes in tax rates. This is the type of system we described earlier in
which a taxpayer's bill depends on the property's relative share of assessed
value.

An alternative system is a *rate-based system* in which tax rates are not adjusted for changes in assessments. In this system, an increase in assessed value
would lead directly to an increase in tax bills. Over time, one would expect rates
to adjust towards the outcome in the budget-based system, but these adjustments
make take considerable time.

As Martin (2008) describes, before Proposition 13, California's property tax
system was a combination of two idealized property tax systems. Consider a
typical county. A property owner in that county would be subject to taxes on his
or her property from multiple and overlapping jurisdictions. The county, city,
school district, mosquito district, and a host of other special districts could each
choose their own tax rate. The total tax rate faced by the property owner would
be the sum of each of the rates chosen by the jurisdiction. There was often no
coordination between these governmental actors and each would have its own
rules for setting tax rates. Some political bodies would be more visible and open
to the public, while others would remain obscure and work in relative anonym-
ity. This was not the idealized town-hall meeting with one rate setting authority
and extensive public comment. It was large, unwieldy and complex.

Another key player in this drama was the elected county assessor. Pressured
by different interests, of varying technical sophistication, political skill, and hon-
esty, and only loosely supervised by the California State Board of Equalization,
these elected officials determined assessments of all nonstate assessed properties
within the county. Commercial and industrial properties were assessed by different methods than residential properties and typically on different cycles.

As long as inflation remained low and property values did not increase dramatically, this jerrybuilt system managed to work. Individual property tax owners might see assessment increases and governmental authorities might raise rates, but there were no wholesale forces undermining the system.

The great inflation of the 1970s and rise in housing prices undermined this system. Now the changes in assessments wrought by the assessors mattered a great deal. As local governmental agencies were not coordinated, inertia often ruled, tax rates were not reduced immediately as assessments soared and local agencies profited and governmental entities often reaped windfalls. In addition, the more frequent assessment of residential property relative to commercial properties engendered a shift in the distribution of the property tax burden towards homeowners. This was exacerbated by newly implemented methods of computer-assisted mass assessments (CAMA) that now became possible through computer technology.

The fall in incomes and property values during the Great Depression undermined the existing property tax system at that time and, as described in Hartley, Sheffrin, and Vasche (1996) set the stage for the birth of the income and sales taxes. Similarly, the great inflation in the 1970s was another tumultuous force, undermining California's state and local fiscal system. The assault on the homeowner was real and, while not inevitable in its precise form, Martin (2008) views Proposition 13 as a last-ditch protective response to an unpredictable and unlegislated increase in the tax burden for homeowners.

Taking Stock: What Options Remain?

With the passage of Proposition 13, California taxpayers abandoned the politically fragmented mixture of budget and rate-based systems of property taxation and moved to a pure rate-based system with strict assessment limits. At least for property taxes, they achieved the Adam Smith goal of certainty in taxation.

But it has not been without costs. The 1% fixed tax rate eliminates local discretion, virtually eliminating connections between tax payments and benefits. Indeed, the fixed tax rate effectively converts the property tax to a statewide tax and severely curbs local discretion. Perhaps, as William Fischel (1989) has argued this is an inevitable outcome of the *Serrano* decision on educational finance. While anti-tax conservatives still applaud Proposition 13, it has had the consequence of shifting spending and taxation decisions to state government, which by its very nature, cannot be as directly responsive to immediate public needs.

Despite these defects, Proposition 13 remains very popular among California voters. Results of a recent Field poll (2008) show that 57% of registered voters would vote again for Proposition 13 today. As expected, a higher proportion of homeowners would vote again for the measure (64%) but even 41% of renters would also vote for it today. A report authored by Mark Baldassare from the

Public Policy Institute of California (2006) with similar findings reflects on its support:

> By a large margin (56% to 33%), likely voters (mostly homeowners) believe that Proposition 13 turned out to be a good thing rather than a bad thing for California. Nearly half (49%) are also comfortable with the fact that Proposition 13 (and rising prices) can make recent homebuyers pay higher property taxes than those who purchased a similar home in the same neighborhood several years before.

Why does Proposition 13 remain popular? As I noted above, the driving factors are certainty in taxation coupled with the knowledge that they will eventually step into their neighbors shoes. As long as they remain in their residence, they will not find their lives disrupted by changes in property taxation. If they choose to move, they understood they will most certainly face a new fiscal reality. That, however, is viewed as a "voluntary" action, in the same way that paying a sales tax on a purchase of a new consumer durable can also be seen as a "voluntary" action. In surveys of tax fairness, sales taxes typically rank relatively high. In the 2008 Field poll cited above, of all the major taxes, when asked what state and local taxes were "too high" the sales tax fared the best. This finding is another application of procedural justice theory—taxpayers are effectively given a voice if they choose to move or to purchase a new consumer durable.

Given the popularity and durability of Proposition 13, are there any reforms that might have salience with the voters? Reformers have typically considered three broad areas: relaxation of the rate limit or voting restrictions, a "split roll" system under which residential and commercial property are treated differently, and gradual relaxation of assessment limitations. Here our focus is only on the property tax aspects of Proposition 13, not the voting requirements it imposes for taxation at the state level.

Proposition 13 prohibits additional *ad valorem* taxes on property but does allow parcel taxes, which levy a fixed sum on each parcel in the community. They require a two-thirds vote and have been successfully used in many communities for libraries and schools. Some reformers have suggested that a supermajority be allowed to impose *ad valorem* taxes as well. With strict assessment limits in place, this would not necessarily be disruptive for homeowners. However, two factors work against this possible reform. First, the parcel tax option—already requiring a two-thirds vote—already exists. Second, potential purchasers of new properties, including existing homeowners, may envision higher rates than 1% levied on the market value of their property as posing too high a burden. If so, there could be unintended consequences. We would certainly not want California residents to circumvent this problem by embracing Florida's recent change to its acquisition property tax that now allows homeowners to carry over their existing assessments to newly purchased residences.

Proposition 13 does not distinguish between residential and nonresidential property. All properties, except state assessed utilities, are subject to the 1% rate and the 2% limit on assessment increases. As Martin (2008) recounts, the established business community, including the California Taxpayers Association, originally opposed the passage of Proposition 13 because they feared adverse fiscal consequences for the state. Other states, for example Florida, that subsequently adopted acquisition value property taxation only applied it to homeowners.

It is difficult to develop an intellectual rationale for extending Proposition 13 to businesses. Large businesses often modify or lease rather than sell and, as a consequence, the increase in underlying land values often goes untaxed. The business community naturally fears a split roll because it would raise their tax burden and potentially leave them vulnerable to additional taxation. Sexton and Sheffrin (2003) estimate that raising assessments on commercial and industrial property to market value while maintaining the 1% rate would yield approximately $3 billion statewide.

A recent Field survey (2008) found mild support for a split roll among California registered voters if the issue was framed as raising taxes on business; it had much stronger support if the split roll was envisioned to lower residential property taxes. The split roll has been on the ballot in California and was defeated. But it was deliberately coupled with a variety of onerous business taxes in order to divert campaign contributions from affected businesses away from other candidates and propositions.

What is surprising, however, is that the public does not have a clear idea that Proposition 13 applies to all properties. A June 2005 Field poll (2005) posed the following question: "As you may know, in 1978 California voters approved Proposition 13, which reduced local property taxes. To the best of your knowledge, did Proposition 13's tax reduction apply only to residential property taxes, only to commercial property taxes, or both?" Only 34% of the respondents correctly said it applied to both residential and commercial property. Since Proposition 13 is a constitutional amendment, any changes would require statewide voter approval. Given the lack of deep rationale, general public unawareness, and the prospect of additional revenue, it is possible that under the right ballot circumstances, a split roll could be enacted.

A final reform would be to relax slightly the 2% assessment increase limitation and raise it, to say, 4%. Other states have higher assessment increase limits, for example Florida's is 3%. How much would this seemingly minor change matter? Table 3 contains estimates of disparity ratios unmodified homeowner property in Los Angeles County for 1975 and 1988 base year properties under both 2% and 4% assessment increase limits. The table is constructed by taking the disparity ratios in 1996 as given and then applying the alternative limits over the next 12 years.

As Table 3 indicates, even over a relatively short 12-year period, the disparity ratios decrease by approximately 21%. Over even longer horizons, the power of compound interest works effectively to lower disparity ratios.

Table 3. Effects of Alternative Assessment Increase Limits in Los Angeles

	2% limit	4% limit
1975 base years	8.06	6.30
1988 base year	2.09	1.64

California taxpayers would be resistant to reforms of this nature even though the impact would be very gradual for existing homeowners. Such a change would have to be coupled with other tax reform measures or desired spending measures to make it effective.

While California's Proposition 13 is often maligned as an unfair tax system, as this chapter has emphasized, all property tax systems exhibit inequities. Combining a split roll with a 1% rate and a modest increase in the assessment limit increases would improve the equity of California's system considerably.

References

Anderson, Nathan B. 2007 "Property Tax Limitations: How, What, Where and Why" *State Tax Notes*, January 15, pp. 93-100.

Baldassare, Mark. 2006. "At Issue: California's Exclusive Electorate." Public Policy Institute of California, San Francisco, at http://www.ppic.org/content/pubs/atissue/AI_906MBAI.pdf. Accessed August 9, 2008.

Campbell, Andrea Louise. 2008. "How Americans Think about Taxes: Public Opinion and the American Fiscal State." Manuscript in progress, available at http://www.law.nyu.edu/colloquia/taxpolicy/papers/08/Campbell_excerpt_Intro_Ch_1_6_March_2008.pdf. Accessed August 9, 2008.

Field (California) Poll. 2005. (machine readable data file) San Francisco, Calif.: Field Research Corporation, June, Field (California) Poll 05-02.

Field Research Corporation. 2008. "Proposition 13 Thirty Years after its Passage." June, available at: http://www.field.com/fieldpollonline/subscribers/COI-08-June-Prop-13-Tax-Matters.pdf. Accessed August 9, 2008.

Fischel, William. 1989. "Did Serrano Cause Proposition 13." *National Tax Journal* 42(4): 465-73.

Hartley, James E., Steven M. Sheffrin, and J. David Vasche. 1996. "Reform During Crisis: The Transformation of California's Tax System during the Great Depression." *Journal of Economic History*, September.

Ledgerwood, Alison, Ido Liviatan, and Peter J. Carnevale. 2007. "Group-Identity Completion and the Symbolic Value of Property." *Psychological Science* 18(10): 873-78.

Lind, E. Allen, and Tom R. Tyler. 1988. *The Social Psychology of Procedural Justice*, New York and London: Plenum Press, 267.

Martin, Isaac. 2008. *The Permanent Tax Revolt: How the Property Tax Transformed American Politics*. Stanford, Calif.: Stanford University Press, 249.

Oates, Wallace. 1999. "Local Property Taxation: As Assessment.," Land Lines, Lincoln Institute for Land Policy 11(3), May.

O'Sullivan, Arthur, Terri A. Sexton, and Steven M. Sheffrin. 1995. *Property Taxes and Tax Revolts: The Legacy of Proposition 13*. New York and Cambridge: Cambridge University Press.

Sexton, Terri A., and Steven M. Sheffrin. 2003. "The Market Value of Commercial Real Property in Los Angeles County in 2002." available at: http://www.iga.ucdavis.edu/Research/CSLT/Publications/MarketValueCommercialRealPropertyPaper.pdf. Accessed August 9, 2008.

Sheffrin, Steven M., and Terri A. Sexton. 1998. *Proposition 13 in Recession and Recovery*. San Francisco, Calif.: Public Policy Institute of California, September, p.110.

Tax Foundation. 2006. Special Report. "2006 Annual U.S. Survey of Attitudes on Tax and Wealth, No. 141, Washington, D.C.: Tax Foundation (April).

Wood, Richard J. 2006. *"Supreme Court Jurisprudence of Tax Fairness."* Seton Hall Law Review 36:421-79.

Zodrow, George. 2006. "Who Pays the Property Tax?" Land Lines, Lincoln Institute for Land Policy 18(2), April.

Section III. Public Finance

Proposition 13 Thirty Years Later: What Has It Meant for Governance and Public Services?

Jean Ross[1]

Critics of Proposition 13 have been accused of suffering from "Chicken Little" syndrome since prior to the measure's passage. While the sky didn't fall after the June 1978 passage of Proposition 13, in large part because the state was able to use its sizeable budget surplus to mitigate the impact on local governments, the measure did produce deep fissures in the fabric of public services and the state's systems of governance. Now, 30 years later as the state faces its longest budget stalemate and, perhaps, most difficult fiscal challenges ever, Proposition 13's chickens are coming home to roost.

The 30-year gap between cause and effect may make it hard for many voters to accept the cause and effect relationship. Most would agree, however, that voters' approval of Proposition 13 marked a sea change in public attitudes toward government and the realities of how California pays for and delivers public services.

Proposition 13 marked the end of what advocates for strong public services and an activist government often consider California's golden era—the era that

---

[1]Jean Ross is the executive director of the California Budget Project, a Sacramento-based nonprofit, nonpartisan policy research group.

built university and highway systems and consistently ranked California among the highest spending states on public schools and other services. The turmoil that began in the 1960s and continued through the 1970s culminated with the passage of a ballot measure that contained a strong undercurrent of the old California implicitly and, often times, explicitly, saying that it no longer wanted to pay for the new California and new, more diverse generation of Californians.

Proposition 13 came about at a time when California was growing and becoming more diverse, and when broader economic trends led to increased income inequality. The increasing diversity of the state crashed head on with Proposition 13's requirement that a two-thirds majority of the state's legislature approve any measure increasing state tax revenues. It is this provision—along with others, such as the shift of authority for dividing up the proceeds of the local property tax dollar to the state, that are often overlooked in analyses that focus on Proposition 13's role as a property tax revolt—that I will argue had the most significant impact on California's policy landscape in the subsequent 30 years.

The supermajority vote requirement for state tax increases, along with additional ballot measures limiting local governments' ability to raise revenues, have left California facing repeated state budget crises and lengthy legislative budget stalemates. Arguably, many voters didn't fully realize what they'd voted for in approving Proposition 13. Many may not have understood that the landmark measure's implications extended far beyond the property tax or that it would give state lawmakers a much greater role in financing and governing local services ranging from schools to roads and courts. Absent the supermajority vote requirement for state tax increases, lawmakers could have and probably would have raised state taxes to make up at least some of the shortfall in revenues caused by the measure's 53% reduction in local property tax revenues.

At least one of Proposition 13's primary proponents did, however, have limiting the size and scope of government as a major motivation. In reflecting on the impact and importance of Proposition 13, Paul Gann noted that, "We want to reduce the size of government. Our ballot measures don't say so in so many words, but that's understood to be on the top of any initiative we put out."

His statement anticipates those of latter-day crusaders for a diminished role of government, such as Reagan budget director David Stockman's call to "starve the beast" and anti-tax crusader Grover Norquist's somewhat more blunt statement that "I don't want to abolish government. I simply want to reduce it to the size where I can drag it into the bathroom and drown it in the bathtub."

Now, 30 years later, California's public sector is dangerously close to drowning in Norquist's bathtub.

Over the past three decades, California's population has grown by more than half and become increasingly diverse, with no single ethnic group accounting for a majority of the state's population. California, along with the nation, is also growing older as the baby boomers begin to grey, with the fastest growth among the oldest—and most costly in terms of public services—Californians.

Conservative lawmakers and pundits point to the lower tax levels of California's golden era by way of arguing that lack of money is not at the heart of the state's fiscal and governance ills. This argument, however, ignores the very real fact that the new California and new Californians place demands on public services that cannot be met by the priorities and spending priorities of our parents' and grandparents' generation.

Public opinion research and analyses of voting trends reveal a vast gulf between the state's older, whiter, and more affluent past and its younger, ethnically diverse, and lower-income future. And many, though certainly not all, of those on the older, white, more affluent side of the divide have demonstrated a reluctance to offer the next generation of Californians access to the same level of public services that were available to those of my generation—the generation educated by California's pre-Proposition 13 public schools and universities—that were once the envy of the nation.

Proposition 13's restrictions on the taxing powers of the state, along with other measures backed by many of the same proponents, provide the mechanism by which a minority of the state's voters and population can exert disproportionate influence on state budget and policy priorities. In a small "d" majoritarian democracy, consensus could and, I believe, would emerge to balance the budget using a combination of prudent spending reductions and modest tax increases.

Ironically, a supermajority vote requirement that pre-dates Proposition 13 may be responsible for the measure's passage. Seeing the threat of Proposition 13 to governance and fiscal structures and fearing the wrath of voters at the ballot box, state lawmakers labored to craft an alternative that would have addressed real and perceived problems with the state's property tax system, albeit with a smaller and more controlled impact on local and state governments. However, the most promising of the potential alternatives failed passage in the legislature, unable to achieve the two-thirds support required by the urgency clause needed to place the measure on the June 1978 ballot. Thus, the barriers imposed by one set of legislative supermajority vote requirements begat even more problems for California in the decades to come.

Proposition 13 has left a profound mark on the state's governance and fiscal landscape. Many, if not most, of the ballot measures locking in certain revenue streams—such as Proposition 1A of 2004, which codifies the fiscal relationship between the state and local governments—or establish constitutional spending priorities—such as Proposition 98 of 1988's school funding guarantee—are the direct descendants of Proposition 13. Proposition 13's supermajority vote requirement for tax increases provides an opportunity for advocates for everything from after-school programs to tough-on-crime sentencing laws to use the initiative process to allocate state resources without having to worry that added responsibilities will lead to higher taxes. Instead, voters continue to impose new financial obligations on a structurally limited—via the supermajority vote—state budget.

Proposition 13 and its progeny characterize the inherent conflict between voters' desire for more and better public services and the resistance of at least some fraction of the electorate to paying for them. Public opinion research suggests that resistance to higher taxes is strongest among the largely older, whiter, and wealthier Californians who disproportionately register and turn out to vote. The largely Republican representatives of these voters are a minority of state lawmakers, but California's two-thirds vote requirements grant them effective control of over the state's taxing and spending policies, trumping the interests and preferences of strong majorities of Californians and the legislators who represent them. In contrast, the spending reductions used to balance the budget in hard times in the absence of the legislature's ability to raise revenues largely falls on the young, the nonwhite, and low- to middle-income Californians, generally represented by Democrats who hold a majority, but not two-thirds, of the seats in the legislature.

In good economic times, Republican lawmakers have gone along with, if not actively supported, the spending policies of the Democratic majority. In many good years' budgets, Republican lawmakers linked support for additional spending with passage of tax-cutting measures, such as in 1998 when lawmakers slashed vehicle license fees while expanding support for health, education, criminal justice, and environmental programs. Such deals may garner short-term support, but set the table for a long-term mismatch between the cost of government and the revenues available to pay for it.

Thirty years after the passage of Proposition 13, the sky still has not fallen. This year, 2008, has brought the state its longest budget stalemate ever and arguably most difficult fiscal challenges to date. I would and do argue that the origins of the current crisis *can* be traced directly back to Proposition 13. California's governments have proved to be resilient over the intervening decades, yet there are growing signs that services are stretched, perhaps nearing the breaking point.

On the one hand there is broad-based, often bipartisan agreement, that substantial levels of public investment are needed to ensure that California is well-prepared to meet the challenges of the future. Governor Arnold Schwarzenegger's Commission on Education Excellence concluded that the state needs $10.5 billion more per year—an increase of about 20%—to provide a quality education to all of California's children. Foundation-supported research identifies an even greater need.

In 2007, the governor and Democratic lawmakers worked together with the goal of dramatically expanding health coverage to uninsured Californians. In the end, agreement proved unattainable. In 2008, the same governor proposed significant policy changes that would result in hundreds of thousands of Californians losing coverage and substantially reduce support for California's already underresourced health care system in response to state's massive budget shortfalls. The contrast between the aspirational and the reality illustrates the gap between what California could be and what it is in a post-Proposition 13 era of governance.

And, at a time when business leaders and policy experts all agree we need more, not fewer, college graduates to meet the challenges of an increasingly globalized and sophisticated economy, the state is scaling back support for public colleges and universities.

Is this the year California reaches the breaking point? On the one hand, there is little evidence that voters are ready to rise up and overturn the 30-year legacy of Proposition 13. On the other, evidence increasingly suggests that the status quo no longer suffices for a new and changing California. In 2008, the state experienced its longest ever budget stalemate, with negotiations over how to close a $15 billion plus budget gap dragging months into the new fiscal year. The primary cause of the delay? The inability to achieve the required supermajority vote for revenues needed to close a gap that no lawmaker of either party deems closeable through spending cuts alone. The length, depth, and magnitude of the current crisis, has prompted many to call for a revisiting key features of Proposition 13, but it is too soon to tell whether voters are ready to heed the call for change.

Chapter 10

Proposition 13 as Fiscal Federalism Reform

Kirk J. Stark[1]

Introduction

The adoption of Proposition 13 by California voters in June 1978 was a defining moment in American politics. What might have turned out to be just another midterm primary election instead came to be viewed as a "political earthquake whose jolt was felt not just in Sacramento but all across America."[2] Howard Jarvis's "holy crusade against taxes" is now commonly seen as a precursor to the Reagan revolution, marking "a radical shift in government priorities, public attitudes and social relationships that is nearly as fundamental in American politics as the changes brought by the New Deal."[3] Quotes like these suggest a place for Jarvis alongside America's political giants, a view some might regard as overstated. Still, anyone interested in American history and politics would do

---

[1] William K. Jacobs, Jr., Visiting Professor of Law, Harvard Law School, Professor of Law, UCLA School of Law.

[2] Stephen Moore, *Proposition 13: Then, Now, and Forever*, The Cato Institute (1998).

[3] Peter Schrag, *Paradise Lost: California's Experience, America's Future* (1994), 9, 132. *See also* Isaac Martin, *The Permanent Tax Revolt: How the Property Tax Transformed American Politics,* Stanford, Calif.: Stanford University Press (2008), 2 (tracing political origins of tax cuts in 1980s and 2000s to tax revolt of 1970s).

well to study Proposition 13. Howard Jarvis may not be a founding father, but like Zelig he seems to turn up again and again on the American political stage, usually shaking his fist.

Yet nowhere is Howard Jarvis's lasting influence more palpably felt than in the Byzantine world of California public finance. This essay uses Proposition 13's pearl anniversary as an opportunity to critically examine Jarvis's fiscal handiwork. My specific interest is in evaluating the measure's effect on California's institutions of "fiscal federalism." In using this term, I mean to make reference to "the division of public-sector functions and finances in a logical way among multiple layers of government."[4] Proposition 13 is of course best known for its dramatic reduction in the property tax and the consequent havoc wreaked upon on California's public sector. Yet along with these changes came a fundamental reworking of the division of fiscal responsibilities between Sacramento and local governments. The theory of fiscal federalism, developed principally by economists working in the area of public finance, has a great deal to say about how fiscal decision-making should be structured in a federal setting. With respect to taxation, the theory of fiscal federalism offers guidance regarding questions of "tax assignment"—or "Who should tax, where, and what?" as the late Richard Musgrave once put it.[5] These are the questions I plan to address in this chapter.

Those familiar with the history of Proposition 13 might balk at the introduction of academic theories to the debate over California's public finances—and with good reason. The evolution of the state's fiscal institutions over the past 30 years owes more to chaos and political happenstance than to reason or logic. But my purpose here is not to provide an inventory of deviations from a pure, logical, and coherent scheme of intergovernmental fiscal relations and then simply propose that matters should be put right according to some textbook formula. Rather, the analysis that follows is offered in the spirit of an article published several years ago by Charles McLure on how tax assignment questions depend on history.[6] McLure began his essay by analogizing the question of "optimal tax assignment" to asking how space travelers landing on Mars would assign taxes to multiple levels of government. "Implicit in this formulation," McLure noted, "is an assumption that fiscal history on Mars…starts when the spaceship lands and taxes are assigned." While such an approach may be useful for purposes of developing a normative theory, McLure observed, "it does not help much to understand why tax assignment is what it is or how it might change in the fu-

---

[4] Richard M. Bird, "Fiscal Federalism," in *The Encyclopedia of Taxation & Tax Policy*, ed. Joseph J. Cordes, Robert D. Ebel, and Jane G. Gravelle, Washington, D.C.: Urban Institute Press (2005).

[5] Richard A. Musgrave, "Who Should Tax, Where, and What?" in *Tax Assignment in Federal Countries*, ed. Charles E. McLure, Jr., Canberra: Centre for Research on Federal Financial Relations, Australian National University, in association with the International Seminar in Public Economics (1983).

[6] Charles E. McLure, Jr., "The Tax Assignment Problem: Ruminations on How Theory and Practice Depend on History," *National Tax Journal* 54 (2001): 339.

ture." For that purpose, a "more useful paradigm . . . might ask how benevolent Martian fiscal experts landing on earth at various points in time would suggest assigning taxes, assuming that they want to help maximize the welfare of the Earthlings living in the particular nation where they land."[7]

Thus, in the pages that follow, I hope to channel the advice of McLure's "benevolent Martian fiscal experts," asking what, if anything, tax assignment theory has to say in the case of the "California Federation" three decades into its experience with Proposition 13. The analysis will focus chiefly on the three major sources of tax revenue for California's state and local governments—the property tax, the retail sales tax, and the personal income tax. While certain other taxes and fees have gained in significance since the adoption of Proposition 13, these three taxes continue to dominate the state's fiscal structure, accounting for nearly 90% of the combined own-source tax revenue of California's state and local government.[8]

Proposition 13 and California Fiscal Federalism

California as a Federation

I begin with the proposition that California—like Canada, Australia, and numerous other countries throughout the world—is a "federation" with political authority divided between a central government and political subdivisions. To be sure, there are many differences between the legal structure of these federations and California's vertical division of governmental responsibilities. To state the most obvious, California is itself (at least since 1850) a subnational unit within a larger federation of states. As a result, its power to tax, as well as that of its political subdivisions, is subject to certain limitations imposed by federal statutory and constitutional law.[9] In addition, California's local governments do not enjoy the same degree of legal independence from the state government as the U.S. states or Canadian provinces do from their respective federal governments. Like local governments in most states, California's cities, counties, and school districts are, for the most part, "creatures of the state" and thus derive their powers, fiscal and otherwise, from state law. Yet despite these differences, the same basic design features that make the U.S., Canada, or Australia a federation are also present within the state of California. For purposes of my analysis, the key characteristic is the vertical division of governmental responsibilities between the center and several geographically defined subdivisions.

Within this hierarchical structure, numerous questions of institutional design must be answered, especially with regard to fiscal matters. In their introduc-

---

[7] *Id.* at 340.

[8] 2002 Census of Governments, State and Local Government Finances by Level of Government and by State, 2001-2002, California (October 2005).

[9] *See, e.g.*, U.S. Constitution, Article I, § 8.

tory essay to a recent volume on fiscal federalism, Richard Bird and François Vaillancourt identify six separate questions concerning intergovernmental finance that every federation must answer:

1. The question of expenditure assignment: who should do what?
2. The question of revenue assignment: who should levy what taxes?
3. The question of vertical imbalance: how should any mismatch between the revenues and expenditures of subnational governments be resolved?
4. The question of horizontal imbalance: to what extent should adjustments be made to minimize fiscal disparities among subnational governments?
5. The question of capital markets: what rules should govern borrowing by subnational governments?
6. What sort of process or institutional framework should be used to decide the answers to the foregoing questions?[10]

Over the past quarter century a vast literature has developed addressing these questions in the context of federations around the world. The recent movement toward greater political decentralization in Africa, Asia, and Latin America has intensified interest in fiscal federalism among scholars and policymakers. To get a glimpse of the explosion of interest in this area, one need only spend a few minutes on Google, where searches for Nigerian, Argentine, or Indian fiscal federalism turn up an avalanche of studies and commentary. For the most part, however, this new wave of interest in fiscal federalism has bypassed the internal fiscal structures of the U.S. states.[11] From the disparate attention given to fiscal federalism reform in Buenos Aires versus Sacramento, one might assume that the Golden State must have already perfected its institutions of intergovernmental finance. As discussed below, however, nothing could be further from the truth.

California Fiscal Federalism, Pre-Proposition 13

Prior to Proposition 13, there was a relatively clear and conventional division of taxing responsibility between the state and its local governments. While Sacramento relied principally on income and sales taxes for state revenue, local governments depended heavily on property taxes. To be sure, there was variation among local governments, as well as among local government types, regarding the extent of reliance on the property tax. For example, in this volume David Doerr observes that "[p]rior to the passage of Proposition 13, property tax rates varied widely between urban areas and other regions of the state."[12] Such

---

[10] Richard M. Bird and François Vaillancourt, *Perspectives on Fiscal Federalism,* Washington, D.C.: World Bank (2006), 2.

[11] For an exception, see Daniel L. Rubinfeld, "California Fiscal Federalism: A School Finance Perspective," in *Constitutional Reform in California: Making State Government More Effective and Responsive,* ed. Bruce E. Cain and Roger G. Noll (1995), 431.

[12] David Doerr, *The Evolution of Proposition 13,* Chapter 5, 72.

variation is of course the hallmark of a decentralized system of government where local political communities are in charge of their own fiscal destiny. Thus, at least with respect to the property tax, California's fiscal landscape was marked by a high degree of local heterogeneity of the sort commonly observed in a decentralized federal setting.

In addition to the property tax, California's local governments have also relied on local sales taxes, both before and after Proposition 13. As in most states, the sales tax first made its appearance in California during the Great Depression as a response to unprecedented reductions in revenue from traditional taxes, most notably the property tax. The state adopted its sales tax in 1933, at an initial rate of 2.5%, later increasing that rate to 3% in 1935. After economic conditions improved, however, the state reduced its tax rate to 2.5%. It was this decision, which took effect on July 1, 1943, that prompted several municipalities to adopt local sales taxes. Sensing an opportunity to fill the fiscal void left by the state's decision to lower its rate, the city of San Bernardino enacted the state's first local income tax in 1943 at a rate of .5%. Several other cities followed suit over the ensuing decade, each of them following San Bernardino's practice of taxing sales taking place within city borders.[13] This "situs rule" is by no means the sole (or best) method available for designing a sales tax in a multijurisdictional setting; however, given the fact that local sales taxes arose from the bottom up, rather than the top down, it is not surprising that the situs approach prevailed. Other approaches, such as taxing sales on a destination basis or allocating sales tax revenues according to some other factor, such as population, would have required greater coordination among local governments or a more direct initial role for the state government.

Not surprisingly, the proliferation of local sales taxes throughout the state prompted complaints among business owners regarding the costs of complying with numerous jurisdictions' sales tax laws. Making the case for state uniformity, the managing director of the California Retailers Association observed that "it is nearly impossible for any large business operation, doing business in many municipalities, to comply with all the sales and use tax requirements, regardless of the intention of the executives to follow the law in all particulars."[14] In 1955, the state legislature responded to these complaints by adopting the Bradley-Burns Uniform Sales and Use Tax Law. Under the terms of the Bradley-Burns law as it currently operates, a uniform 1% tax is added to the state sales tax rate and the revenues from that add-on tax are remitted to the city (or unincorporated portion of the county, as the case may be) in which the sale took place.[15] In other

---

[13] For a very useful discussion of the structure and origins of the Bradley-Burns law, see Paul G. Lewis and Elisa Barbour, *California Cities and the Local Sales Tax*, Public Policy Institute of California (1999).

[14] Pierce, "California Has a Sales Tax Headache," *Nat'l Tax J.* 6 (1953): 168, 171.

[15] Beginning with fiscal year 2004-2005, as a result of the so-called "triple flip" legislation, the Bradley-Burn add-on tax is .75% and the remaining .25% is directed to the state; however, cities are reimbursed for the lost revenues via transfers from the "Education Revenue Augmentation Fund" (ERAF). According to state controller data released in

words, the Bradley-Burns legislation left in place the situs approach, first adopted in San Bernardino, of assigning the revenues from the add-on tax on the basis of where the sale took place.

Despite the common reference to the Bradley-Burns 1% tax as a "local" tax, one might reasonably question the use of that term. The tax is administered by the California State Board of Equalization, and its base and rate are entirely a function of state law. In addition, the amount of revenue accruing to any city or county can be (and has been) changed by state legislation, though the state's ability to do so has been limited by a recent constitutional amendment.[16] An alternative term that more accurately captures the substantive effects of the law might be "revenue-sharing" or "tax sharing." Under this view, the Bradley-Burns legislation is nothing more than a decision by the state government to increase its sales tax by 1%, combined with a system of intergovernmental transfers that directs payments to cities and counties based on the amount of taxable sales occurring within each jurisdiction. Of course, at some level, reframing the matter this way is nothing more than a question of semantics. On the other hand, viewing Bradley-Burns as a revenue-sharing arrangement, as opposed to a partial assignment of the sales tax to local governments, brings into sharper relief the fact that the "situs rule" is merely one of many revenue allocation methodologies that the state could adopt with respect to the proceeds from the 1% Bradley-Burns sales tax. As discussed in further detail below, this issue has gained in significance in the years following the adoption of Proposition 13.

Finally, as noted above, the income tax has been used exclusively by the state government in California. While the state began taxing the income of corporations in 1929, it did not adopt a personal income tax until 1935, becoming the 28th state to adopt such a tax. Like the sales tax that came two years before it, the California income tax is a product of the Depression-era overhaul of the state's fiscal structure.[17] Yet unlike the sales tax, there was no effort by local governments to climb aboard the state's new personal income tax. Instead, state law specifically preempted local income taxes, providing that no local government "shall levy or collect or cause to be levied or collected any tax upon the income, or any part thereof, of any person, resident or nonresident."[18] As a result of this provision, which remains in the law today, the income tax has long been the exclusive domain of the state government within the state's fiscal structure.

Thus, the basic arrangement of taxing responsibilities prior to Proposition 13 was (1) income taxes to the state government, (2) property taxes to local gov-

---

early 2008, approximately 21% of total city general fund revenues came from sales and use taxes for 2004-2005. John Chiang, California State Controller, Cities Annual Report, Figure 1, page vi (May 16, 2008).

[16] Proposition 1A, discussed further *infra*.

[17] James E. Hartley, Steven M. Sheffrin, J. David Vasche, *Reform During Crisis: The Transformation of California's Fiscal System During the Great Depression*, Journal of Economic History 56 (1996): 657.

[18] California Revenue and Taxation Code, section 17041.5.

ernments, and (3) sales taxes shared between state and local governments according to terms established under state law.

Proposition 13's Tax Assignment Effects

Proposition 13 fundamentally transformed these tax assignment decisions. It did so most directly by specifying state constitutional restrictions regarding the operation of the property tax. The centerpiece of the reform was a rollback of assessed valuations to 1975-1976 levels, along with a limitation of the tax rate to a maximum of 1%.[19] Thereafter, assessed valuations would be allowed to increase by only 2% per year. Only in the case of a "change in ownership" (usually a sale or other disposition of the property) would the assessed valuation of the property be adjusted upward to its fair market value.[20] In combination, these provisions constituted an unprecedented centralized regulation of the local property tax. Of course, Proposition 13 is rarely described this way. Most view it as a grassroots populist revolt against the political establishment.[21] Even granting the accuracy of this characterization, however, Proposition 13's indisputable effect was to introduce a rigid, top-down regulation of what was previously a locally controlled tax. Whereas prior to Prop. 13 property tax burdens were largely a function of local political choice, after the measure passed nearly every vestige of local fiscal autonomy with respect to the property tax had been eliminated and fixed by state constitutional law.

The basic framework described above is well known and provides the bulk of Proposition 13's substantive tax limitation bite. However, an additional provision within Proposition 13, hardly commented upon at the time of its enactment, cemented the reassignment of the property tax from local governments to the state. Although the property tax continues to be "collected by counties" (as specified by Proposition 13 itself), the revenues derived through the imposition of the tax must be "apportioned according to law to the districts within the counties."[22] According to an opinion from legislative counsel regarding the effect of

---

[19] For purposes of issuing bonds for the acquisition or improvement of real property, local governments may issue bonds the repayment of which may be made from property tax revenues derived from rate increases beyond Proposition 13's 1% limit. These bonds must be approved by a two-thirds majority of the locality's voters. California Constitution, Article XIIIA, section (b)(2). For school construction bonds, the approval threshold is 55%. California Constitution, Article XIIIA, section (b)(3).

[20] California Constitution, Article XIIIA, section 2(a). Since the adoption of Proposition 13, the state has developed detailed rules concerning what does and does not constitute a "change of ownership" triggering a reassessment. Note that Proposition 8, which passed in 1979, permits a downward adjustment to fair market value in the absence of a change of ownership.

[21] For an alternative view, see Daniel A. Smith, "Howard Jarvis, Populist Entrepreneur: Reevaluating the Cases of Proposition 13," *Social Science History* 23 (1999).

[22] California Constitution, Article XIIIA, section 1(a).

this provision, the phrase "according to law" would be interpreted to mean that the state legislature has the authority to decide how property tax revenues are to be divided among local governments.[23] Here again, then, we see further evidence of Proposition 13's centralizing influence. Instead of local communities determining the magnitude of property tax flows into local government coffers, these decisions are now made in Sacramento.

How the state legislature has gone about allocating property tax revenues in the 30 years since Proposition 13's passage is itself a fascinating political story. In the immediate aftermath of Proposition 13, the state legislature enacted SB 154, which, among other things, established a temporary methodology for the allocation of property tax revenues among local governments. A year later, the legislature amended these allocation provisions via AB 8, a highly complex set of rules that effectively directs property tax revenues to the various local governments within any county in accordance with each government's share of property tax revenues prior to Proposition 13's passage.[24] Yet because Proposition 13 gives the state legislature the power to control the allocation of property taxes, these rules have been regularly revisited and revised, most commonly when the state government finds itself in difficult budgetary circumstances. In effect, by giving Sacramento ultimate control over the flow of property tax revenues, Proposition 13 enabled the state government to meet its own financial needs by altering the division of property taxes among local governments. By allocating a greater share of property tax revenues to schools and away from cities and counties (via the so-called "Educational Revenue Augmentation Fund" or ERAF), the state has reduced its own fiscal obligations with respect to K-14 financing. The opportunity for such shenanigans has been limited by Proposition 1A, adopted in November 2004, adding yet another layer of complexity to the centralized regulatory structure inaugurated by Proposition 13. Thus, in every substantive respect California's property tax is now a *state* tax. The rate and base of the tax are specified in state (constitutional) law while the distribution of property tax revenue is a function of state (statutory and constitutional) law. As one author recently explained, "the combination of these provisions effectively eliminated the property tax as a tool of local government revenue generation, centralizing authority over the property tax in state government."[25]

From the perspective of tax assignment theory, Proposition 13's removal of the property tax from local governments to the state government is an unfortunate development. In many ways, the property tax is an ideal local tax. The bulk

---

[23] Legislative Counsel, Opinion 17388 (December 29, 1977).

[24] For a useful overview of the allocation issue, see David Doerr's chapter in this volume. See also Therese A. McCarty, Terri A. Sexton, Steven M. Sheffrin, Stephen D. Shelby, "Allocating Property Tax Revenue in California: Living with Proposition 13," *National Tax Journal* 71 (2005); David G. Ellege, *Demystifying the California Property Tax Apportionment System: A Step-by-Step Guide through the AB 8 Process* (2006).

[25] Christopher Hoene, "Fiscal Structure and the Post-Proposition 13 Fiscal Regime in California's Cities," *Public Budgeting and Finance* (Winter 2004): 51, 54.

of the property tax base consists of real property, which is largely immobile—at least in the short term. Among the principles that animate the basic theory of fiscal federalism is the idea that local governments should not be assigned tax bases that can easily escape the jurisdiction of local tax authorities. For example, few would suggest that corporate income taxes should be assigned to local governments. A system of local corporate income taxes could be easily avoided by corporations relocating to localities that promise a lighter tax burden. In effect, because of the availability of "exit" as an additional tax avoidance strategy, the elasticity of the corporate income tax base is much higher with respect to local corporate income taxes than it would be for state, federal, or global corporate income taxes. Corporate locational decisions would be distorted by a local corporate income tax, yet little or no revenue would be collected. It is with good reason that local corporate income taxes have no champions among public finance analysts.

By contrast, there is general agreement among public finance theorists that property taxes are suitable for local government use.[26] The case for local property taxes is best understood by focusing on the land component of the property tax base. Because land is immobile and fixed in supply,[27] the opportunities for avoiding a land tax are quite limited as compared to other types of taxes. This happy picture is complicated to some degree by considering forms of property other than land, such as the buildings that sit on top of land. While physical structures are certainly less mobile than most other types of property, interjurisdictional variation in property tax burdens can, over time, lead to distorted investment decisions, with property owners more likely to improve or rebuild structures in jurisdictions with lower property tax rates. Still, by comparison to the alternatives, the property tax holds up well as a tax for use by local governments.

Another advantage of assigning property taxes to local governments concerns the positive feedback loop between local government officials and local property owners. This view of the property tax has been developed principally by economist William Fischel. As Fischel notes, under a system of local property taxes where the base of the tax is the property's fair market value, local government officials have an incentive to craft local policies that maximize the value of local property since doing so augments the local tax base. One might say that local political representatives are "rewarded" (either through increased

---

[26] See, e.g., Enid Slack, "Alternative Approaches to Taxing Land and Real Property," in *Perspectives on Fiscal Federalism*, ed. Richard M. Bird and François Vaillancourt (2006), 197-98, discussing advantages of assigning property taxes to local governments under the theory of fiscal federalism.

[27] At first blush, it may seem completely obvious that land is fixed in supply; however, local zoning laws can influence the supply of land available for alternative uses. Thus, while land itself may be fixed in supply, various subcategories of land, such as land available for residential construction or land available for commercial development, will likely increase or decrease in supply over time as a result of changes in local land-use regulations.

revenues or opportunities to claim credit for lowering tax rates without lowering revenue) by policies that have the effect of increasing the value of local property. Likewise, local property owners have less of an incentive to oppose increased local property taxes when those revenues are put to some local use that could enhance their property values. In effect, a system of *local* property taxes, where the base of the tax is the fair market value of the property, puts property owners and local government officials in partnership with one another. Each wants to see the other succeed, at least insofar as "success" is defined as the adoption of local government policies that work to maximize local property values. At least in some sense, therefore, the property tax has characteristics of a "benefit tax," making it an appropriate tax for local government use.

The centralization of the property tax is the chief tax assignment effect of Proposition 13, but it is not the only one. There have been numerous other changes to the local fiscal landscape in the 30 years since the passage of Proposition 13, including the proliferation of miscellaneous fees, assessments, and special taxes as local governments have looked for innovative financing schemes to circumvent the fiscal confines of Proposition 13. Some of those changes are arguably positive developments according to the standard theory of fiscal federalism, such as the increased reliance on user fees as a source of local public revenue. To the extent that these fees reflect the marginal cost of providing a government service, such as trash collection, their use would be consistent with the general insight that local governments should rely, wherever possible, on price-like financing arrangements, leaving redistributive taxes to higher levels of government. But of course because of the nature of public goods, the availability of price-like user fees is likely quite limited. For example, it is not clear how a user fee would be crafted for certain core local government functions, such as police and fire protection.

One additional effect of Proposition 13 on California fiscal federalism deserves mention. As noted above, the 1955 Bradley-Burns legislation established the 1% local add-on to the state sales tax. As a legal matter, therefore, this local revenue source predates the adoption of Proposition 13 by nearly a quarter century. In practice, however, the new constitutional limitations on the property tax put greater pressure on the sales tax as a source of revenue for local governments, especially cities. This indirect effect of Proposition 13 has manifested itself in two important ways.

First, cities hoping to raise additional revenue have more readily turned to the sales tax after Proposition 13 than before. Of course, because the tax rate and the legal definition of the base are specified as a matter of state law, there is only one way for a city to increase local sales tax revenues—i.e., to attract a larger base to the jurisdiction. As a result of the situs rule, according to which revenues from the Bradley-Burns tax are directed to the jurisdiction where the sale takes place, an increase in local sales tax revenues requires an increase in the number of taxable sales occurring within the city. Not surprisingly, then, cities hoping to bolster their sales tax receipts have made every effort to attract large "sales tax generators" such as car dealerships, outlet malls, and various big box retailers like Wal-Mart and Home Depot. According to a California Senate Local Government Committee report issued in 1989, the "incentive is so strong that cities and counties actually attempt to 'steal' sales tax generators from other localities."[28] As anyone with even a passing familiarity with California public finance will testify, competition for sales tax generators is a statewide phenomenon. But some of the most fascinating stories come from the pitched battle among Oxnard, Ventura, and Camarillo along the Highway 101 corridor from Los Angeles to Santa Barbara, an area colorfully portrayed as "Sales Tax Canyon" in William Fulton's book, *The Reluctant Metropolis*.[29]

A second and perhaps less obvious effect of Proposition 13's limitations on the property tax is the degree to which it has made the fixed pot of Bradley-Burns sales tax revenue a more highly coveted asset in the ongoing fiscal struggles between Sacramento and California's cities. The effect has been most evident during times of budgetary stress, when the state government, strapped for cash, has looked to revenue sources normally devoted to local governments as a means of augmenting state revenues. A noteworthy example is the so-called "triple flip" mechanism used in the 2004 budget deal, which diverted .25% of the Bradley-Burns "local" sales tax for purposes of repaying state bonds that helped to cover the state's budget deficit. While the triple-flip package incorporated a property tax shift to cities and counties to compensate them for the loss of sales tax revenue, the deal understandably made local governments nervous about the reliability of the Sacramento's long-term compensation promises. It was that nervousness that prompted local governments to push for the adoption of Proposition 1A, a constitutional amendment passed in November 2004 to restrict the state's ability to reduce revenue streams currently dedicated to local governments. The larger lesson here concerns the evisceration of local fiscal autonomy in California since the adoption of Proposition 13. With every major tax now effectively controlled by Sacramento, local governments have turned to the state constitution as the battleground for protecting existing revenue streams.

Tax Assignment Reform under Prop. 13 Constraints

To return to McLure's analogy raised at the outset of this essay, we are now at the point where the "benevolent Martian fiscal experts" have arrived to offer an evaluation of California's institutions of fiscal federalism. There is no blank slate, no turning back the clock or wishing that Proposition 13 had never happened. Even 30 years later, Proposition 13 continues to enjoy widespread popu-

---

[28] Senate Local Government Committee Report (1989) cited in Lewis and Barbour, *supra* note 13 at 12 (1999).

[29] William Fulton, *The Reluctant Metropolis: The Politics of Urban Growth in Los Angeles*, Baltimore: Johns Hopkins University Press (2001).

lar support.[30] This basic political fact suggests that Proposition 13's key provisions will remain constitutionally entrenched for some time to come. Thus, it would appear that, for the time being at least, the only fiscal federalism reforms that are even potentially on the table are those that can exist within the constitutional architecture of Proposition 13. This is not to suggest that constitutional reforms should not be considered or that Proposition 13 should be regarded as politically sacrosanct. To be sure, there are many worthwhile reforms that could be pursued. For purposes of this analysis, however, I want to regard the basic Proposition 13 framework as a binding political constraint. Given these constraints, what sort of tax assignment reforms might be advisable for California going forward?

The Likely (Continued) Ossification of Property and Sales Taxes

The first point to be made is that there is very little room for constructive reform of the property tax without amending the state constitution to modify the basic provisions of Proposition 13. While several innovative property tax reforms have been advocated in recent years, such as the adoption of a split-roll system that would preserve Proposition 13 protections only for residential real estate, these reforms typically require constitutional amendments. While some of these reforms may be politically viable in the future, the likelihood of any meaningful reworking of Article XIIIA at this time seems very low. By making this observation, I certainly do not mean to underestimate the value of giving serious consideration to possible reforms of the California property tax; however, the long-term political durability of Proposition 13 militates against viewing the property tax as a source of meaningful fiscal federalism reform.

Unfortunately, present arrangements for the sales tax are also not a likely avenue for reform, but for somewhat different reasons. As discussed above, the California sales tax, including the Bradley-Burns "local" add-on, is fundamentally a state tax with a built-in rule directing a portion of revenues to the jurisdiction where the sale takes place. While the situs rule can and should be abandoned in favor of an alternative allocation of Bradley-Burns revenue, perhaps one based on population rather than the physical location of retailers, doing so would require a constitutional amendment because of the adoption of Proposition 1A in November 2004. Again, it bears emphasizing that such constitutional reforms are deserving of serious consideration, especially since in the case of reforming the allocation of Bradley-Burns revenue the electorate's political instincts are surely not as set in stone as they seem to be with respect to property tax reforms. Nevertheless, in keeping with the basic spirit of this essay to respect

---

[30] *Proposition 13 Thirty Years After Its Passage*, California Opinion Index (June 2008) ("Statewide more than twice as many voters (57%) report that they would vote in favor of Proposition 13 if it were up for a vote again today as would vote against it (23%).").

the stated constitutional preferences of the California voters, I will assume that modifications to the sales tax's situs rule are, for the time being at least, politically off limits.

The Possibility of Local Income Taxes

In contrast to the property and sales taxes, there are relatively few legal barriers to reform of California's individual income tax. Section 26(a) of Article XIII of the California Constitution provides that "taxes on or measured by income may be imposed on persons, corporations or other entities as provided by law."[31] Thus, the state legislature has the authority to allow local governments to impose income taxes. Under current law, however, local governments are prohibited from relying on income taxes. Section 17041.5 of the California revenue and taxation code provides as follows:

> Notwithstanding any statute ordinance, regulation, rule or decision to the contrary, no city, county, city and county, governmental subdivision, district, public and quasi-public corporation, municipal corporation, whether incorporated or not or whether chartered or not, shall levy or collect or cause to be levied or collected any tax upon the income, or any part thereof, of any person, resident or nonresident. This section shall not be construed so as to prohibit the levy or collection of any otherwise authorized license tax upon a business measured by or according to gross receipts.[32]

As noted above, the effect of this provision has been the assignment of the income tax to the exclusive use of the state government. Should this longstanding approach be abandoned and the statute amended to allow cities, counties, or school districts the power to impose their own local income taxes? Several states have recently amended their laws to allow local income taxes, to the point that one might almost label this a trend in U.S. subnational taxation. In addition, numerous foreign countries, including most notably the Scandinavian countries, have long relied on local income taxes. In considering the advisability of such a reform for California, several important points need to be kept in mind.

First, under the terms of Proposition 13 and Proposition 218, the "Right to Vote on Taxes" initiative passed by California voters in November 1996, any local income tax would require approval by voters in the jurisdiction imposing the tax. If the tax were proposed as a "general tax"—defined as "any tax imposed for general governmental purposes"—simple majority voter approval would be required. If the tax were proposed as a "special tax"—defined as "any tax imposed for specific purposes"—two-thirds voter approval would be re-

---

[31] California Constitution, Article XIII, section 26(a).
[32] California Revenue & Taxation Code, section 17041.5.

quired.[33] These provisions, which are a product of the ongoing evolution of California's fiscal constitution since 1978, pose a potentially significant barrier to the adoption of local income taxes should state law be amended to permit them.[34] At the same time, however, the constitutional requirement of voter approval leaves open some political space for an expansion of local fiscal autonomy within the parameters of Proposition 13. One might even say that Proposition 13 envisions (or at least does not preclude) local autonomy with respect to nonproperty taxes, *provided there is voter support for such taxes.*

Second, in extending the authority to impose income taxes to local governments, policymakers would face certain basic design decisions, including most importantly the choice between a residence-based and source-based system of income taxes. Under a residence-based approach, local governments would be permitted to tax only their own residents, whereas under a source-based system localities would also be allowed to tax income earned in the jurisdiction by non-residents (with a credit mechanism used to avoid taxing the same income twice). There are many reasons to prefer a residence-based approach under principles of fiscal federalism. Most importantly, a residence-based income tax limits the opportunity for communities to export tax burdens to nonresidents, increasing the likelihood that local tax burdens reflect local preferences for public spending rather than just a desire to increase public spending at the expense of outsiders. From a political perspective, however, it seems likely that representatives of the state's large employment centers (e.g., Los Angeles, San Francisco) would lobby for a broader power to tax the income of nonresident commuters.[35]

Finally, in allowing local governments to impose income taxes, consideration should also be given to the possible adoption of some type of equalization system to minimize the adverse effects of interjurisdictional disparities in income tax capacity, especially under a regime of residence-based local income taxes. Given the considerable income segregation in the state, taxable resources available to some jurisdictions would greatly exceed those available to other jurisdictions. The availability of lower tax prices in some jurisdictions (due to higher incomes) could create an incentive for fiscally induced migration and corresponding efficiency losses. A properly designed system of intergovernmental grants could mitigate these effects by reducing the relative fiscal advantage enjoyed by higher-income communities.

---

[33] California Constitution, Article XIIIC.

[34] The development of California's fiscal constitution from Proposition 13 through Proposition 218 is discussed at length in my article, "The Right to Vote on Taxes," *Northwestern Univ. Law Review* 96 (2001): 191.

[35] Note that both Los Angeles and San Francisco have relied on payroll expense in the calculation of their business license taxes. San Francisco continues to impose such a tax at a rate of 1.5% of payroll. The Los Angeles payroll expense tax was repealed, effective January 1, 2002. See Antoinette Christovale, *Business and Other Taxes,* Office of Finance, City of Los Angeles, (January 2005) (available at http://www.lacity.org/finance/pdf/INFOBKLE.pdf).

Conclusion

It should be clear that the foregoing discussion has provided only the most general overview of Proposition 13's impact on California fiscal federalism. No attempt has been made to provide a detailed discussion of all taxes available to state and local governments. By limiting my analysis to the state's three major sources of revenue—property taxes, sales taxes, and income taxes—I have attempted to highlight the basic structural transformation that Proposition 13 worked on the division of taxing authority between California and its political subdivisions. As discussed above, the dominant effect has been a significant transfer of power to Sacramento and a corresponding reduction in local fiscal autonomy. At some level, these developments call into question the very idea of local government. If cities, counties, and school districts exist primarily to carry out state policy functions in a manner determined in Sacramento, then the decline of local fiscal autonomy since the adoption of Proposition 13 is of no moment. However, if local governments exist at least in part to allow the state's diverse political communities to make independent choices regarding the nature and amount of local public goods they wish to consume, then some effort should be made to give local governments the fiscal autonomy to achieve those ends. The dilemma for policymakers is how to promote local fiscal autonomy within the very restrictive parameters of Proposition 13.

Proposition 13 Thirty Years after the Revolution: What Would Howard Jarvis Say?

Joel Fox[1]

Proposition 13 coproponents Howard Jarvis and Paul Gann were not around to celebrate the measure's 30th anniversary. They were senior citizens when the measure was on the 1978 ballot. Jarvis passed away in 1986, Gann in 1989.

Jarvis was the more visible and recognizable of the two proponents, indeed it was Jarvis who appeared on the cover of *Time* magazine after Proposition 13 passed. For his efforts in leading the Proposition 13 fight, Jarvis was even named a runner-up as *Time* magazine's man of the year.

Since he is not here, we have to wonder what Howard Jarvis might say as Proposition 13 reached its 30th anniversary.

I suspect he would say Proposition 13 did the job he intended it to do. People are secure in their homes because property tax is controlled. And, he would argue Proposition 13 has not shortchanged government. He always claimed to have talked to experts about the acquisition property tax system (in which assessments on the property are determined at the time of purchase with a set in-

---

[1] Joel Fox operates *Joel Fox Consulting*, a public affairs/political consulting firm. He also currently serves as president of the *Small Business Action Committee* and is a co-publisher and editor-in-chief of the website *Fox and Hounds Daily* (www.foxandhounds daily.com), which offers commentary and news on California business and politics.

crease allowed for inflation gain). Jarvis said the experts told him when houses and commercial property were resold and reassessed at market value, along with new construction; government would receive increasing and adequate revenue.

One thing that would not surprise Jarvis is that a legion of critics is still trying to knock down his masterwork. He would undoubtedly use some colorful language to push back against his critics as he always did. "Popcorn balls" was a favorite expression. I'm not sure what that meant, but political discourse has displayed much more outrageous epithets over the years.

What would please Jarvis most of all would be the realization that few homeowners are threatened by unmanageable property taxes. I remember how he would marvel at the homes stretching in all directions as the airplane he traveled on slowly came in for a landing at LAX, and he would say, "I sure saved a lot of people their homes with Prop. 13."

If Jarvis were here today, he would look at places like Silicon Valley where a few years ago a converted garage sold for about $1 million and be satisfied that the small three-bedroom house down the street from the converted garage did not see an unconscionable increase in its property taxes.

He might remember reading about the elderly couple that was written about in the *Newhall Signal* newspaper about a decade before Proposition 13 passed. The couple lived in a small shack, which was assessed at the land's highest and best use—a motel could be built on the property. The couples' taxes were $1,800 a year; their total income was $1,900 a year. And he would smile, puff on a cigar, and know people like that could not be victims of an unsympathetic tax system again.

And what would he say about the criticism Prop. 13 receives? He'd wave a fist and call it hogwash, or something more colorful.

I will not be so dismissive here. I will discuss Proposition 13 thirty years later. I will touch upon the criticisms of Proposition 13; and also what Prop. 13 has accomplished for the people of California. And if Howard has a word or two to offer along the way, I'll be sure to let him speak.

Proposition 13 has suffered many attacks over the years. In Ancient Egypt plagues came from the hand of God. In California all problems seem to be blamed on Proposition 13.

Prop. 13 has been blamed for poor government services, missing shot puts, (when the grass is too high because it is not cut often enough), potholes, fee hikes, even a murdered child. The writer Richard Reeves argued in a *Money* magazine piece that 12-year-old Polly Klaas may have been rescued by the police before she was killed if officers had compatible police radios surely denied them by the Prop. 13 tax cuts.

When the Loma Prieta earthquake collapsed freeways in the San Francisco Bay Area in 1989, Paul Conrad's *Los Angeles Times* editorial cartoon showed a car crushed by a freeway and the license plate on the car read: Prop. 13.

When O. J. Simpson was found not guilty in his criminal trial, a column in the *New Republic* said it was Howard Jarvis and Prop. 13's fault. Because of the tax cut there was not enough money to hire competent police officers and coroner officials. As they say in advertisements . . . that's just a partial list.

Once again in the year 2008 we have a budget crisis in California. And once again hungry eyes turn to Proposition 13 and wonder if only . . . if only we could blow it up; or trim it back; or give it a face lift; or get away from the Neanderthal instincts of its supporters. . . . California will be rescued.

In other words, if taxes could be easily raised spending would be increased and problems would be solved.

It is curious that Proposition 13 is blamed for budget deficits but is never given credit when there are budget surpluses and healthy economic growth that has occurred over the years since the initiative passed.

In the conclusion of Bill Stall's May 29, 2008 *Los Angeles Times* column on Prop. 13, he called for changes in the measure so that taxes might be raised. He concluded: "But make no mistake, it is Proposition 13—because of its real impact on state coffers and its iconic role as a tax revolt symbol—whose reform is the crucial first step in assuring California's future."

Its iconic role as a tax revolt symbol—What he means is to increase taxes in California the symbol of tax resistance must be torn down.

He's right.

Proposition 13 is legendary. It was more than a simple tax revolt. Proposition 13 as a symbol contains elements of the myths and legends with which we grew up.

Consider the story of Robin Hood. Think beyond the simple notion that he took from the rich and gave to the poor. Look deeper. He took from those who became rich through outrageous taxation. The villains in the story were Prince John, the head of the national government and the sheriff, tax collector for the local government.

If you are not inclined toward romantic tales, then consider Proposition 13 as a social movement, providing for the taxpayer security in their housing. At the same time Prop.13 provided stability to neighborhoods and a sense of power in the people that they do, indeed, control their government.

The symbolism of Prop. 13 is powerful. And that is why some need to tear it down.

Three decades later, both as a taxpayers' shield and as a symbol of power over government, Proposition 13 still enjoys overwhelming support from the public. Three different voter surveys issued at the time of the 30th anniversary conducted by Mark DiCamillo of the Field Poll, Mark Baldassre at Public Policy Institute of California, and Arnold Steinberg of Arnold Steinberg and Associates all agreed that Proposition 13's popularity maintained the same two-to-one margin of approval the measure passed by in 1978.

Let us consider briefly some familiar policy issues raised about Proposition 13:

- The two-thirds vote requirement to raise taxes
- Taxing commercial property and residential property the same
- Shifting power to the state government

- The fiscalization of land use (in which cities look to bring in sales tax producing retail establishments and, it is alleged, forego good planning for the sake of sales tax revenue)
- Schools
- Tax equality

The Two-Thirds Vote

Proposition 13 changed the law requiring a two-thirds vote for the legislature to raise state taxes and a two-thirds vote of the people to raise local taxes for special purposes. Proposition 13 is not responsible for the two-thirds vote requirement to pass the state budget or to pass local general obligation bonds. Both of those requirements predate Prop.13 by many years.

The two-thirds vote for local general obligation bonds was established in the 1879 constitutional convention. The two-thirds vote on the budget was first established in 1933 for budgets that exceeded 5% growth over the previous year's budget. The two-thirds standard was applied to all state budgets after the constitutional revision of 1962.

However, these two issues, bonds and budgets, make the point that a supermajority vote is often required in certain instances when the people believe that hurdle is appropriate. The two-thirds vote can be found many times in the United States Constitution. Juries require a supermajority vote, in some cases a unanimous vote, to convict. Simply stated the two-thirds vote is to bring a sense of overall agreement to important decisions. In taking property in the form of taxation it is appropriate to cross this hurdle.

Split Roll Property Tax

The question was asked of Howard Jarvis why he didn't write Proposition 13 to protect only homeowners. He was accused of writing Proposition 13 to benefit business. Business organizations actually opposed Proposition 13 when it was on the ballot and contributed money for its defeat.

Jarvis did not believe Proposition 13 was a special favor for business. He stated that for 50 years the state constitution had the same tax rate and requirements for business properties and residential properties and if business got a break under Proposition 13 those properties had been getting the same break for 50 years.

Splitting the property tax roll to assess or tax business property differently from residential property will have negative effects both politically and economically for the business community.

Once business property is on a different footing than residential property business is susceptible to future tax increases, which will be hard to fend off. As the old saying goes, "Business doesn't vote." Business property tax could be subject to ambitious politicians or special interest groups looking for more revenue.

Once the roll is split it can be spliced many different ways as has happened in other states, i.e., commercial plants, store fronts, even boat docks. Interest groups will constantly lobby for favored status under such a system.

Business organizations actually use Proposition 13 as a selling tool to businesses wanting to relocate in California. Why? Under Proposition 13 they argue that a business can plan better, knowing what property taxes will be each year and that the business will no longer be subject to the uncertainty of subjective tax bills from an assessor.

Finally, taxing business will send a ripple effect through the economy. The tax will be passed on in the form of higher rents to small business, and increased prices on goods and services.

Power to Sacramento

Has power shifted to Sacramento under Proposition 13? What would Howard Jarvis say? He defended the phrase in Proposition 13, which states that the tax revenue should be "apportioned according to law." In his mind that meant dispersing the tax money as it had been dispersed in the past along the same lines. The legislature interpreted the phrase to mean that *we make the laws so we will say how the money is spent.* State government control over the property tax is not foreign to California. The state controlled property taxes in the beginning of statehood. But, the legislature did use the language of Proposition 13 to take more power unto itself and at times direct where property tax revenue would be spent. Some power has shifted to state government. That was not Jarvis's intent.

Fiscalization of Land Use

Governments use a divining rod to find more revenue. If their way is blocked in one direction, they will dig somewhere else. With property taxes limited by Proposition 13, cities certainly have approved the building of retail establishments to secure more sales tax revenue, a situation that has been termed "the fiscalization of land use." Some Prop.13 critics have charged that this desire to chase sales tax producing outlets has skewered appropriate land-use decisions. But businesses do not build outlets to satisfy a need to build. Companies probably do more polling than most politicians to determine if a specific area is a good market for their goods and services. And that means that most citizens in the area probably are pleased that these outlets are located near them. If Proposition 13 were to disappear there would still be a need and a call for the retail outlets.

While land-use decisions may be made differently if Proposition 13 did not exist, the remedy for this situation seems to be to raise property taxes, and voters have clearly expressed their views on that idea.

Schools

There is more money in the school system today than prior to Proposition 13. There are certainly more students in the schools than there were in 1978, the year Proposition 13 passed. And yet, for each student, in real per capita dollars, more money is spent on the students. A study by the Center for Government Analysis pegged that figure at 30% more per pupil.

So where is the money going and how is it being spent? Study after study shows education is not just about money. Too much administration, union rigidity, parental involvement or lack there of are all issues. And the problem is not just in California. Consider the following paragraph. It was written 17 years ago, so keep that in mind when you read the dollar figure of $12,000 per pupil—that was a lot of money 17 years ago, even more than is spent on California students today, but the complaint is familiar.

> In our town, the school system is spending just over $12,000 a pupil. That should make it roughly the elementary equivalent of Stanford. Instead, people who are able to send their children to private and parochial schools because they believe the public schools are substandard. This makes us like many other urban residents in the country. The cupboard is bare, and taxpayers everywhere are looking around to see where the money has gone. And the answer, in so many cases, is that it has been badly spent.

So wrote Anna Quidlen, in the *New York Times* in 1991 commenting on schools in New York City where there is no Proposition 13.

There are many problems with public education in this country that do not revolve around money.

Tax Equality

Property tax was not and is not a fee-for-service. It is a general fund tax. Characterizing it as anything different is wrong. Prior to Proposition 13 when garbage was picked up in front of the expensive house on top of the hill, the cost of that pick up was the same as the house at the bottom of the hill. But the property tax system in place at the time required the higher assessed house to pay more yet the service was the same.

The question of tax equality under Proposition 13 occurs when similar homes in the same neighborhood pay different tax amounts depending on the assessed value determined when the homes were purchased. The issue of equality of taxation must be measured against the question of certainty for the tax-payer.

All taxpayers are treated equally when they set their property taxes at the sales price under Proposition 13. The perceived inequality comes later when a new buyer comes into the neighborhood and that buyer's taxes are adjusted according to the current assessed value of the property. At least all the taxes in the neighborhood would not increase dramatically because someone decided to buy a house at a high price, a situation that existed before Prop.13.

The United States Supremes Court in the case of *Nordlinger v Hahn* (1992) dismissed the notion that Proposition 13 violated the equality clause of the U.S. Constitution. Justice Harry Blackmun writing for the eight to one majority argued:

> First, the state has a legitimate interest in neighborhood preservation, continuity and stability. . . . Second, the State legitimately can conclude that a new owner at the time of acquiring his property does not have the same reliance interest warranting protection against higher taxes as does an existing owner, already saddled with his purchase, does not have the option of deciding not to buy his home if taxes become prohibitively high.

At the Howard Jarvis Taxpayers Association offices people who called to complain about paying more taxes than their neighbor who lived in an identical house stopped calling after a few years. They saw how Prop.13 was working for them keeping their taxes certain despite the turnover of homes in the neighborhood.

An acquisition property tax policy makes taxes predictable and removes the problem of subjective assessments by government officials, while protecting homeowners against prohibitive property tax increases. Taxpayers know that their property taxes will be 1% of the market value, in most cases the purchase price, and in the future would go up no more than 2% a year.

Adam Smith stated in his *Wealth of Nations*: "The certainty of what each individual ought to pay is, in taxation, a matter of so great importance, that a very considerable degree of inequality . . . is not near so great an evil as a very small degree of uncertainty."

Proposition 13 captured Smith's notion of certainty.

Or as a writer in the *Vacaville Reporter* described the situation of side-by-side similar homes paying different tax amounts: Proposition 13 reminded her of her grandmother's quilt. It was made up of different patches but stitched together it kept everybody warm.

Before Proposition 13 passed, the certainty in property taxes belonged to the tax collector. After Proposition 13, the certainty in property taxes belongs to the taxpayer. *That is the revolutionary idea behind Proposition 13.*

Thirty years after the passage of Proposition 13 the debate on its merits still rages. This would not surprise Howard Jarvis. He formed the taxpayer group that now bears his name because he knew Prop.13 would not stand if it were not protected. He supported continuous advocacy on behalf of the taxpayers. As Howard would say: "A ship can't sail on yesterday's wind."

It's interesting to note that over the past year around the country there was outrage over property taxes in many states. Indiana saw protests and picketing of the governor. The situation in Florida was covered in *Time* magazine. Property tax initiatives were filed in Arizona, Washington, and Nevada . . . but in California there was property tax peace. People were satisfied with the system.

One other thing—the property tax has been the most reliable tax in California, growing steadily year after year. Revenue from property tax does not fluctuate with changes in the economy as does income tax and sales tax revenue. In Los Angeles County, since 1980, property tax revenue has gone up by an average of 7% a year. Even with the housing market crisis of 2008, county officials reported property tax increased 6.9%.

The headline story of the July 9, 2008 *Los Angeles Times* said it all: "Property Tax Funds Rise as Housing Market Falls."

The story indicated that assessors throughout California were reporting rising tax bases and "they credited the 30-year-old law (Proposition 13)—revealing its unexpected role as an economic stabilizer."

Because properties are assessed at their selling price instead of the current market value and subject to limited inflation increases, even when home prices dip most properties continue to pay their current taxes plus an increase due to the inflation factor. Thus even in difficult economic times taxes calculated on a home, unless recently purchased, go up not down. This allows for the tax revenue stabilization cited by the *L. A. Times*.

What would Howard Jarvis say? Given that he had many battles with the *Times* over tax policy, seeing the paper's front page headline story reporting a positive worth of Prop.13, he might be speechless.

Is Proposition 13 a perfect law? No, there is no perfect law.

Oliver Wendell Holmes said the life of the law is not logic but experience. Proposition 13 resulted from the experience of California taxpayers over many years when the government, instead of offering taxpayers relief from an ever-increasing property tax burden, did nothing.

Proposition 13 did not actually cut off money to government as some have charged. On Proposition 13's 30th anniversary, the *San Diego Union Tribune* editorialized:

> From fiscal 1980–81—the year Proposition 13 took effect—through 2005–06, property tax revenue skyrocketed from $6.4 billion to $38.3 billion. That is an increase of more than 500 percent. So much for talk that the measure turned off the property tax spigot.
>
> Any claim that the two-thirds requirement to hike state taxes depressed other revenue is also flat wrong. Total state revenue went from $19 billion in 1980–81 to $93.5 billion in 2005–06—a jump of nearly 400 percent.
>
> These whopping revenue gains occurred in an era in which the state's population went up by 58 percent and, according to federal data, inflation rose by 131 percent. The upshot: Lawmakers have at least twice as much money—inflation-

adjusted money—to spend per Californian as they did when Proposition 13 took effect.

Perhaps, the best summary of Proposition 13's effect may have been expressed in a *Los Angeles Times* editorial on the occasion of Proposition 13's 20th anniversary.

Proposition 13 is 20 years old and it's time to proclaim the tax cutting measure a success. The ballot brainchild of Howard Jarvis and others has been vilified by critics for two decades and blamed for much of what ails California. But at the heart of it, the measure did exactly what Jarvis promised. More important, it fulfilled the demands of California homeowners, many of whom legitimately feared that runaway property taxes would force them from their homes.

And Howard Jarvis would say: "Damn right!"

About the Authors

David Doerr, Chief Tax Consultant, California Taxpayers Association. Doerr served 24 years as Chief Consultant for the Assembly Revenue and Taxation Committee and is widely recognized as the foremost expert on California's *Revenue and Taxation Code*. His institutional knowledge of California's tax structure is unparalleled. Doerr is the founding editor of *Cal-Taxletter*, and the author of *California's Tax Machine: A History of Taxing and Spending in the Golden State*, published in 2000.

Jack Citrin, Heller Professor of Political Science and director of the Institute of Governmental Studies, UC Berkeley. Citrin is a scholar of political behavior and comparative politics whose publications include *Tax Revolt: Something for Nothing in California* (Cambridge: Harvard University Press, 1982, 1985), co-authored with David Sears and *California and the American Tax Revolt* (Berkeley: University of California Press, 1983), as well as various articles on initiative politics in California. *Tax Revolt* is the authoritative text on the Proposition 13 vote, and remains a keystone of the literature on public opinion concerning taxing and spending.

Mark DiCamillo, senior vice president of Field Research Corporation and director of *The Field Poll*, an independent, nonpartisan, media-sponsored survey of California public opinion. As a senior member of Field Research's professional staff, DiCamillo directs a wide range of market and opinion research projects for foundation, media, government, and institutional clients. As director of *The Field Poll*, DiCamillo measures California voter preferences in all major statewide candidate elections and ballot proposition contests in California. He is the author or co-author (with Mervin Field) of over eight hundred separate reports on public opinion, assessing political, economic, and social trends in California and state politics. DiCamillo is a *cum laude* graduate of Harvard University and holds an MBA from Cornell University's Johnson School of Business.

William Fischel, professor of economics, Dartmouth College. Fischel has written extensively about local government, property taxation, and school finance, most recently in *The Homevoter Hypothesis* (Harvard University Press, 2001). His hypothesis that court-mandated school finance equalization caused Proposition 13 has been widely noted. He has been a visiting professor at UC Davis and UC Santa Barbara and a visiting scholar at UC Berkeley Law School. Fischel's book, "Making the Grade: The Economic Evolution of American School Districts," is under contract at the University of Chicago Press.

Joel Fox serves as principal of Joel Fox Consulting, a public affairs/political consulting firm located in Granada Hills. Fox also currently serves as president of the Small Business Action Committee, founded in 2003 to battle for small business on important political issues. In May 2008, Fox launched *Fox and Hounds Daily*, a website that discusses the mix of business and politics in California, and he serves as its editor-in-chief. Fox was with the Howard Jarvis Taxpayers Association for 19 years, serving as the president from 1986 to 1998. He is an adjunct professor at Pepperdine University Graduate School of Public Policy and the author of *The Legend of Proposition 13* (2003 Xlibris).

John Fund, a columnist for the *Wall Street Journal*, writes the weekly "On the Trail" column for OpinionJournal.com. He is author of *Stealing Elections: How Voter Fraud Threatens Our Democracy* (Encounter, 2004). Fund joined the *Journal* in April 1984 as deputy editorial features editor. He became an editorial page writer specializing in politics and government in October 1986 and was a member of the *Journal*'s editorial board from 1995 through 2001. Fund worked as a research analyst for the California State Legislature before beginning his journalism career in 1982 as a reporter for the syndicated columnists Rowland Evans and Robert Novak. In 1993, he received the Warren Brookes Award for journalistic excellence from the American Legislative Exchange Council.

David Gamage, assistant professor of law, Boalt Hall, UC Berkeley. Gamage is currently finishing a two-part project analyzing how state tax systems should respond to fiscal volatility and the resulting budget crises. Previously, he taught at the University of Texas at Austin School of Law as an Emerging Scholars Program Assistant Professor. Gamage has a J.D. from Yale, where he served as a senior editor on the *Yale Law Journal* and as a Law and Economics Fellow. Additionally, he has an M.A. in economic and organizational sociology from Stanford, as well as a B.A. in economics from Stanford.

Isaac Martin, assistant professor of sociology, UC San Diego, author of *The Permanent Tax Revolt: How the Property Tax Transformed American Politics* (Stanford University Press 2008), an award-winning book that traces the political impact of the property tax revolt in California and beyond.

Jean Ross, executive director, California Budget Project. The California Budget Project is an independent Sacramento-based think tank that engages in independent fiscal and policy analysis and public education with the goal of improving public policies affecting the economic and social well-being of low- and middle-income Californians. She previously served as principal consultant to the California State Assembly's Revenue and Taxation Committee and serves on the board of the Washington, D.C.-based Institute on Taxation and Economic Policy; the advisory board of the Tax Policy Center, a joint project of the Urban Institute and Brookings Institution; and the advisory committee of California's Franchise Tax Board.

Terri Sexton, professor of economics, California State University at Sacramento. Sexton is the co-author, with Arthur O'Sullivan and Steven Sheffrin, of *Property Taxes and Tax Revolts and Proposition 13 in Recession and Recovery*. She has also written numerous articles on Proposition 13 and its impact on the local public sector.

Steven Sheffrin, professor of economics and director of the Center for State and Local Taxation at UC Davis. Sheffrin has been a visiting professor at Nuffield

College (Oxford), the London School of Economics, and Princeton University. He has also served as a financial economist with the Office of Tax Analysis and the U.S. Department of the Treasury. He has served as a member of the board of directors of the National Tax Association. His books include *Property Taxes and Tax Revolts: The Legacy of Proposition 13* (Cambridge University Press, 1995, co-authored with Arthur O'Sullivan and Terri Sexton) and *Proposition 13 in Recession and Recovery* (Public Policy Institute of California, 1998, with Terri Sexton).

Kirk Stark, professor of law, UC Los Angeles. Stark has written extensively on state and local tax policy, with a particular focus on issues of "fiscal federalism"—the allocation of fiscal responsibilities among federal, state, and local governments. He is the co-author with Jonathan Zasloff of "Tiebout & Tax Revolts: Did Serrano Really Cause Proposition 13?" 50 *UCLA Law Review* 801-58 (2003). He has been a visiting professor at Harvard Law School and has served as a member of the board of directors of the National Tax Association.